columbus
WAS first

by

MICHAEL A. MUSMANNO

Introduction by

John B. Duff, Ph. D.

Associate Professor of History
Seton Hall University

Fountainhead Publishers, Inc.
475 FIFTH AVENUE, NEW YORK, N. Y. 10017

AUTHOR'S ACKNOWLEDGMENTS

Appreciation is warmly expressed to all those who kindly assisted me in the preparation of this book, the authors of the various works consulted, columnists of newspapers and current periodicals referred to during my studies of this subject. Gratitude is expressed particularly to those who assisted me with information at Yale University: Mr. Alexander O. Vietor, Curator of Maps of the Yale University Library; Dr. Thomas E. Marston, Curator of Medieval and Renaissance Literature, for the facilities afforded me as well as for the courtesies shown on my two visits to the Beinecke Rare Book and Manuscript Library to study the Vinland Map, the Tartar Relation and that part of the Speculum Historiale at the Library.

My appreciation is extended for quotations from ADMIRAL OF THE OCEAN SEA by Samuel Eliot Morison reprinted by permission of Atlantic-Little, Brown and Company Publishers, copyright 1942 by Samuel Eliot Morison; to Admiral Morison together with his agents Curtis Brown, Ltd. for permission to quote from his monumental work THE OXFORD HISTORY OF THE AMERICAN PEOPLE.

Appreciation is due for permission to quote from THE PROBLEM OF WINELAND by Halldor Hermannsson, copyright 1936 by Cornell University; used by permission of Cornell University Press; as well as quotations from THE VINLAND SAGAS by the same author, copyright 1944 by Cornell University, used by permission of Cornell University Press.

Permission was graciously given to me to quote from their

respective books as identified in the text by the following authors: THE NORSE DISCOVERIES AND EXPLORATIONS IN AMERICA by Edward Reman published by University of California Press; THE NORSE ATLANTIC SAGA by Professor Gwyn Jones published by the Oxford University Press; THE VOYAGES OF THE NORSEMEN TO AMERICA by William Hovgaard published by The American-Scandinavian Foundation; THE JOURNAL OF CHRISTOPHER COLUMBUS published by Clarkson N. Potter, Inc.

Appreciation is due the Yale University Press for permission to quote from THE VINLAND MAP AND THE TARTAR RELATION by Skelton, Marston and Painter in which the Vinland Map appears and which is reproduced in this book by specific permission of the Yale University Press; CHRISTOPHER COLUMBUS by Salvador de Madariaga published by The Macmillan Company; Penguin Books Ltd for permission to quote from their publication THE VINLAND SAGAS, translators M. Magnusson and H. Palsson.

I also thank all those not specifically mentioned for help and encouragement, the patient staffs of the historical libraries visited and especially my publishers, Fountainhead Publishers, Inc., Director Mrs. Rose P. Portugal, for the skillful assistance rendered by their editors Arthur Portugal and Frances Diane Robotti.

"I had six honest serving men—they
taught me all I knew—their names were
Where and *What* and *When* and *Why* and *How*
and *Who*."

Rudyard Kipling (1865–1936)

INTRODUCTION

When I first saw the title of the manuscript which Justice Musmanno was kind enough to let me read, I was somewhat apprehensive. Remembering the furor occasioned by the publication by the Yale University Press of *The Vinland Map and the Tartar Relation,* I feared it would be a cataloguing of testimonials to Columbus and rebuttals of Leif Ericson dutifully presented by a prominent jurist with a strong ethnic bias and a cavalier disregard for facts. My fears were unfounded. Justice Musmanno has delivered a wholly serious, albeit irreverent, challenge to the authenticity of Yale's well-publicized map.

The question of whether any Europeans reached the shores of America in the centuries before Columbus cannot fail to fascinate all of us, whatever conclusions we reach. It may well be, as Washington Irving said in his epic biography of the great Genoese navigator:

"A wandering bark may occasionally have lost sight of the landmarks of the old continents, and been driven by tempests across the wilderness of waters long before the invention of the compass, but never returned to reveal the secrets of the ocean . . ."

But, Washington Irving adds:

"Certain it is that at the beginning of the fifteenth century, when the most intelligent minds were seeking in every direction for the scattered lights of geographical knowledge, a profound ignorance prevailed among the learned as to the western regions of the Atlantic; its vast waters were regarded with awe and wonder, seeming to bound the world as with a chaos, into which conjecture could not penetrate, and enterprise feared to adventure."

Christopher Columbus dared to pierce conjecture and possessed the faith and courage to embark on the adventuresome risk that had held fast the anchors of the boldest mariners and thus solve a problem that had baffled the wisest men of the age.

No one can possibly question that the westward sweep of European colonizers which followed the revelation of that October day in 1492 began the greatest migration in history. As Samuel Eliot Morison proclaimed in his magisterial biography, *Admiral of the Ocean Sea:* "The whole history of the Americas stems from the Four Voyages of Columbus." The nations that turned their gaze across the Atlantic, in the wake of the great Italian's discoveries, dominated for centuries thereafter the history not only of this continent but of their own.

None of these considerations, of course, affect the issue of the genuineness or spuriousness of the Vinland Map, the presentation of which, via the mass information media, seems to have been the immediate inspiration of this book. I suspect that this book will provoke a good deal of debate over the map's importance and authenticity. Should this map turn out to be a traveler with a false passport, a Cardiff giant of cartography, Justice Musmanno's work will have played the role of prime mover in the unmasking. In any event, *Columbus WAS First* will force its readers to think about and possibly reevaluate some fundamental historical concepts, a healthy phenomenon.

It is not my place to evaluate the technical arguments pro and con the Vinland Map, but I would like to make one observation. Intending no disrespect to the academic world of which I am an inhabitant, I nevertheless find it refreshing to see a well-publicized and widely accepted theory, based on intensive research carried on under the aegis of a great seat of learning, wittily and cogently challenged by an outsider, a nonacademician—although, as a graduate of five universities and a jurist as well as an author of note, Justice Musmanno is well qualified as a scholar of distinguished competence. Make no mistake about it, he is a thoroughgoing Columbus partisan with little patience for those who prefer the esoteric, the unverified, the hypothetical view of history. Herein lies much of the charm of the book. Anyone who has ever felt intimidated by a footnote or temporarily silenced in debate by his opponent's citation of eminent authority, will be grateful to Justice Musmanno for his demonstration of what a single angry man, armed with as much analytical skill as conviction, can do to puncture what he feels is an ill-launched balloon of erudition.

John B. Duff, Ph. D.
Associate Professor of History
Seton Hall University

June 1966
South Orange, New Jersey

LETTER FROM H. R. TREVOR-ROPER

Excerpts from letter received by Justice Musmanno from H. R. Trevor-Roper, distinguished author, Regius Professor of Modern History, Oxford University, England:

"Thank you for sending me your book COLUMBUS *WAS* FIRST. I have read it with interest and I entirely agree with you. I have not examined the actual manuscripts at Yale, and therefore cannot comment about the wormholes which are so essential a part of the editors' arguments, but I regard it as an elementary rule in all such matters that anyone who produces a disconcerting manuscript puts himself under an obligation to reveal, with the manuscript, as far as possible, the antecedent history of the manuscript. Mr. Witten's refusal to do this seems very difficult to justify, and he has only himself to blame if sinister explanations fill the vacuum of information.

"As to the (Vinland) map, the whole thing seems palpably fishy . . . If there is any authority in the world which I would accept without question on such a subject, it is that of Eva Taylor (Professor Emeritus of Geography, University of London), a splendid lady, as full of common sense as of scholarship."

CONTENTS

Contents

Part I

THE VINLAND MAP

Chapter 1

HOLIDAY FOR WORMS

This book has been written in answer to the question: who discovered America?

That a book should have to be written to make the point that Christopher Columbus discovered America may seem inconceivable to some; to others, brought up on or converted to the more "sophisticated" view that Leif Ericson discovered America, it may seem rather quixotic. It is my hope that those of this latter frame of mind who read this book will come away with a better idea of upon just what sort of evidence the claim for the Viking discovery of our continent is actually based. It is my further hope that the analysis of this evidence in the later chapters—including the evidence of the glamorous new "surprise witness," the Vinland Map—will lead some of these readers to reevaluate their preconceptions.

So long as there are theorists who dress the legend-enshrouded figure of Leif Ericson with the mantle of Finder of America, so long as archaeological ambiguities and maps of dubious pedigree are flaunted as new "proofs" of their theories by the daily press, so long as these "proofs" are accepted unquestioningly by a large portion of the public, satisfied that the "experts" have spoken—then I feel that this book has its *raison d'etre*.

And a third group of readers—those who are honestly confused by the headline-grabbing derogations of Columbus and no longer know what to believe—will, I hope, find herein material to help clarify the subject.

The solid historical foundation on which Christopher Columbus stands as the discoverer of America has been undermined—according to an antiquarian bookseller and the champions of a "Vinland Map" recently published by the Yale University Press—by five worms. These worms, by eating their way through sheets of parchment and heavy paper, establish, say the champions of the map, that a section of the northeastern region of North America had entertained a European settlement some five centuries before the western sun gilded the prows of the *Santa Maria,* the *Nina,* and the *Pinta.*

The Capitoline geese, we have been led to believe, honked out a warning of the Gallic invasion to the ancient Romans, a spider led Robert Bruce to victory, Mrs. O'Leary's cow kicked over the lantern which started the Great Chicago Fire . . . and now, are these variously talented beasts to be joined in the Ark of Legend and Lore by Yale's five little crawlers?

Those of us who have accepted that authenticated history, and unquestioned documentation prove Columbus and only Columbus the true discoverer of America, now find ourselves faced with the necessity of examining the credentials of these worms for their newly-assigned role as sappers of established fact, and of reviewing the plausibility of the arguments of those who have cast the worms in such an unaccustomed role.

We will return later to these worms and what they are supposed to prove and how they are supposed to prove it, but first let us consider the end result of their epochal appetites: headlines. Headlines such as WORMHOLES IN MAP FILL GAP IN NORSE HISTORY; MAP PUTS VIKINGS FIRST IN AMERICA; VIKINGS DID BEAT COLUMBUS; VIKINGS, NOT COLUMBUS, SAW N. AMERICA FIRST. And when did these headlines appear? Columbus Day, 1965.

How did all this come about? What startling coincidence caused the map referred to in the headlines to break into print on Columbus Day? A number of days before October 12, 1965, the Yale University News Bureau sent out to newspapers throughout the country a release which specifically carried the embargo: "This story cannot be released publicly until Monday, October 11." The release then proclaimed "The dramatic discovery of the only known map, showing the New World lands discovered by Leif Ericson long before Columbus." A few paragraphs later the release revealed that the Yale University Press had a book to sell, *The Vinland Map and the Tartar Relation,* reproducing the map and the ancient manuscript with which it was bound, with articles by the three scholars who had worked on their identification. And then, with an outright gratuitous sneer at Columbus, the release informed the world that "The Vinland Map will go on public display at Yale in the Beinecke Rare Book and Manuscript Library starting Tuesday, October 12—Columbus Day."

The Associated Press began its story on the Vinland Map announcement with these melancholy words: "Yale University scholars sliced the frosting off Christopher Columbus's birthday cake today." The Philadelphia *Inquirer* said editorially: "Yale University scholars have chosen a rather back-handed way to celebrate Columbus Day, by displaying what they regard as documentary proof that the Genoan did not discover America." In an editorial printed the same day, the New York *Herald Tribune* said: "There is a good deal of irony in the fact that the Yale University publication of a pre-Columbian map showing the New World (in much abbreviated form), with a tribute to the explorations of Bjarni and Leif Ericson, should have been announced on the eve of Columbus Day."

Even *Izvestia,* the official organ of the Soviet government, had to put in its two rubles: "The importance of this discovery would be hard to overestimate."

And overestimate it is just what many of us did not do, after rinsing the bad taste of the Columbus Day timing of the Yale announcement from our mouths and extricating our thoughts from the choking ivy tendrils of august academic "authority." The announcement, after all, was not prepared by Yale's history faculty nor was it necessarily reflective of a consensus of their opinion.

Yale's broadside at the *Nina,* the *Pinta,* and the *Santa Maria* had been fired, the smoke had begun to clear. Voices began to be heard, voices of those who did not, indeed, overestimate the importance of the news story of the day. New York's

Mayor John V. Lindsay, himself a Yale graduate, in the midst of his mayoralty campaign, declared:

> "I majored in history at Yale and I know right from the horse's mouth, Columbus discovered America . . . Saying Columbus didn't discover America is as silly as saying Di Maggio doesn't know anything about baseball, or that Toscanini and Caruso were not great musicians, or that LaGuardia was not a great mayor of New York."

New Jersey's United States Senator Clifford P. Case declared: "Leif Ericson is just an upstart, as far as I'm concerned." Governor Richard J. Hughes of the same state said: "Yale to the contrary, I'm glad to be here to honor Columbus." And New York's Governor Nelson Rockefeller stated: "As far as the impact of Columbus' voyage is concerned, he discovered America."

In Washington, Representative Richard D. McCarthy of New York rose in Congress to call the Yale announcement "in poor taste on the eve of Columbus Day." He added: "All the maps in the world will never diminish his fame."

And the editorial pages of the newpapers began to bristle with indignant rejoinders to the cavalier manner in which Columbus was being treated by the New Haven publicity. The New York *Daily News* in an editorial: "If it's all the same to Yale, or even if it isn't, we'll continue to regard Columbus as this hemisphere's real, result-getting discoverer."

And the New York *Journal-American:* "Let the eggheads, in their cloistered researches, have their respective heroes. Back in our dear old school days Christopher was a good enough discoverer. Let's not go changing finders in the middle of the stream of time."

John La Corte, Founder and Director of the Italian Historical Society of America, New York City, said: "Columbus discovered America, and we will dispel Yale's claim very fast." He then asked: "Could not this map have been introduced in a dignified manner through a geographical or historical world

medium whereby an impartial and broad evaluation could have
been given?"

And the distinguished historian Samuel Eliot Morison,
twice a Pulitzer Prize winner for his biographies of Christopher
Columbus and John Paul Jones, was also surprised at the press-
agentry surrounding the publication of the map. In his review
of *The Vinland Map and the Tartar Relation* for the New York
Times Book Review, he observed:

> "Ordinarily a literary or historical discovery is mod-
> estly announced by an article or two in some learned
> journal. This one, however, has been fluffed up into a
> quarto of 259 pages, plus index, etc. (106 for Tartar
> Relation and the rest for Vinland Map), and the latter
> has received an amount of publicity more appropriate
> for the discovery of a lost Gospel or the Dead Sea
> Scrolls than for a mid-15th-century map containing an
> island called 'Vinland.' "

One may be incensed by the tastelessness of commercializ-
ing Columbus Day by using its celebration as the publicity
springboard for proclaiming the sale of a map and an accompanying book purporting to reduce the stature of Columbus in
history. One may find it comparable perhaps to using Washington's Birthday to publish and publicize a whitewashing biography of Benedict Arnold. One may have a natural inclination to
cling to the values imparted to us in school days, and regard the
celebrated Genoese as the discoverer of the Western lands,
whatever fruitless landfalls any Vikings may or may not have
made. But scholarly arguments can only be answered by scholarly arguments. Has more than skepticism, indignation, and
nostalgia been marshaled against the imposing walls of erudition behind which the Vinland Map is sequestered?

Yes! The voice of scholar has been raised against scholar,
the pen of expert crossed with that of expert. The arguments of
the Yale authorities have been answered with arguments by
other authorities. One at a time, as they have had a chance to

evaluate the evidence (and not waiting for Eli Yale's birthday to make their announcements), noted researchers in the various academic disciplines involved in the controversy have voiced their doubts about the authenticity and significance of the Vinland Map.

In the February, 1966 issue of *Encounter* (London), G. R. Crone, Librarian and Map Curator of the Royal Geographical Society, London, in a review of the Yale University Press's book under the heading *How Authentic Is the "Vinland Map"?*, writes: "With every respect for the erudition displayed, I consider the authors have set too high a value on this Map." Crone advances detailed arguments to support his view that the map "is probably post-Columbian" and its depiction of Vinland "not of exceptional significance."

The March 6, 1966 issue of the *Sunday Times* of London headed an illustrated article occupying most of a page "Is the Vinland Map a Forgery?" Among other criticisms of the map's authenticity, the *Times* mentions a paper by the renowned British geographer, Professor Eva Taylor, summarized in the Institute of Navigation Journal, and to which I will refer later.

And *Newsweek* took notice of the growing controversy in its issue of April 11, 1966 ("The Map Flap"), outlining some of the points made both by the map's supporters and by those who regard it, as *Newsweek* puts it, as "a cartographic Piltdown man."

Undoubtedly between this writing and the reader's happening upon it, more criticism will be offered, perhaps raising points that cannot be anticipated in the present volume. One can only hope that all those who were vaguely persuaded that somehow (who knows how?) the Vinland Map proved that Columbus did not discover America, will learn, our mass news media willing, that the last word on the subject has by no means been said.

It seems all too true that rumor outruns refutation. But not always. In 1911–12 there was found in Piltdown, England, a skull which some anthropologists claimed belonged to prehistoric man of the Pleistocene period (some 10,000 to 25,000 years ago). In 1915 there was unearthed close by a fossil lower jaw supposed to match up with the skull. The Piltdown Man was talked about everywhere as a "great find." In 1953 British scientists proved it to be a brazen forgery. The skull was demonstrated to be modern, and the jawbone an ape's.

If the breath of healthy skepticism can gain the public's ear with only half the success with which Yale's five little worms crawled their way onto the front pages of America's newspapers, then I am confident that a fair-minded public will have no difficulty in deciding who is entitled to be called the Discoverer of America.

In the following chapters of this volume I propose, using the arguments of authorities on all sides of the controversy as well as arguments for which I am solely responsible, to demonstrate that:

The Vinland Map, because of the secrecy surrounding its purchase, the ignorance of its past and genealogy, and innate fallacies demonstrable on its face, cannot be used to prove the pre-Columbian arrival of Norsemen in America; and that:

The Norse sagas, on the sole evidence of which the Viking "discovery" of America had been hypothecated prior to the revelation of the "proof" of the Vinland Map, are a series of folk legends so intertwining the real and the fanciful, so self-contradictory and vague and ambiguous, and so lacking in adequate confirmation, that nothing deserving the name of proof can be based upon them to support the theory of the Viking primacy.

And, finally, I propose to remind my readers of the size and nature of the achievement of Columbus, the magnificent scope and purpose of his undertaking and the supreme qualities of mind and character that so well fitted him for it. . . . With my apologies to those readers who have no need to be reminded, even in these days of debunking, of who discovered America, and how and why.

Chapter 2

YALE BUYS A MAP

How did the five little worms wriggle into the spotlight of historical controversy?

The story begins in the year 1957 when Laurence Witten, a New Haven, Connecticut, dealer in antiquarian books, maps and manuscripts, purchased, somewhere in Europe, an old map and an old manuscript, with wormholes in them, the two items bound together in a nineteenth-century binding. The manuscript was an account, not first-hand, of the expedition of Friar Carpini to the land of the Mongols in the mid-thirteenth century, in itself a document of interest only to a limited number of specialists. Certainly there was nothing about this Tartar Relation, as it has been called in Yale's publication, that would cause its existence to come to the attention of the general public.

The undated map, a sheet of parchment about 11 by 16 inches with a single fold, depicted rather crudely the earth, ringed by the sea, a medieval conception of the earth. There were a recognizable, if distorted, Europe, rough guesses at Asia and Africa, and an assortment of islands, real and imaginary. Nothing out of the ordinary so far . . . but, in the upper left-hand corner, to the left of Iceland, was the unmistakable outline of Greenland, properly labelled, and to the west and south of Greenland a large, rather bizarre island designated Vinland. Vinland is one of the names given in the Norse sagas to the land supposed to have been reached by Leif Ericson and others in the tenth or eleventh century, and has been identified by different writers with Newfoundland or various parts of the north-eastern North American mainland. The curiously shaped island on the map certainly does not look anything like America or any part of America, and if one were guided merely by what one saw, without reading the inscription or having been exposed to the publicity barrage that announced the map, it is inconceivable that one would identify this island with any existing geographical entity.

Above the grotesquely formed land appeared in Latin the words: "Island of Vinland, discovered by Bjarni and Leif in company." Another Latin legend read: "Eirik, legate of the Apostolic See and bishop of Greenland . . . . . arrived in this truly vast and very rich land . . . . . in the last year of our most blessed father Paschal, remained a long time in both summer and winter . . . . ."

Since Pope Paschal II died in January, 1118, this would presumably date the arrival of the Greenland Bishop in Vinland some time in 1117. If, then, this strange terrestrial mass were to be accepted as truly representing North America, the argument could be made from the map that the western hemisphere had been inhabited some 375 years before Columbus sailed. Ergo, this would demonstrate that the Genoese navigator was really a late-comer to our shores and that it was not he who had drawn aside the veils of obscurity to reveal a new world to a startled mankind. If the map were genuine, if it were drawn before Columbus sailed, and if its attribution of the name "Vinland" rested on a solid geographical basis, it would indeed be a monumental discovery!

History, because of this map, would have to be rewritten, the Norse legends and the speculations based upon them would be transmuted by this philosopher's stone of parchment into the pure gold of fact. And, naturally, the map would become one of the most priceless documents of all time. But objects called "priceless" for aesthetic or historical reasons—great paintings or significant manuscripts—do change ownership from time to time, and when this happens some price must be agreed upon. All of these considerations affected the transaction that was eventually to take place between Laurence Witten and the anonymous donor who purchased the Vinland Map from him for presentation to Yale. *Time* magazine, in its issue of October 15, 1965, said: "The price paid is a closely guarded secret, but it was admitted to be 'in the high six figures,' or in the neighborhood of $1,000,000." The Columbian devotees can take some comfort in the thought that the price for attempting to dispossess Columbus from his place in history was indeed a fabulous one.

But in 1957 Laurence Witten found himself faced with a dilemma: how could he prove that this map really depicted a pre-Columbian discovery of America? A number of features of the map, *prima facie*, rebelled against this interpretation. Most obvious of them was that the outline called Vinland, as I have mentioned, did not in the least resemble North America or any segment of it. Its identification rested solely on the inscription referring to the Norse legends and to its position on the map where the northeastern corner of North America would have been had North America been on the map. But all Witten saw southwest of Greenland was a squiggle looking like a child's drawing of a one-eyed ogre with a greedy, devouring mouth. (It was later to be asserted, in Yale's Columbus Day press release, that the ogre's eye represented Hudson Straits, the mouth the Gulf of St. Lawrence.)

A second obvious difficulty was the outline of Greenland: it was too good, too pat for such an ostensibly ancient map. It was almost as if a quarto of a "lost" play by Shakespeare were to turn up, but with a scene in which the hero jumps into a car and drives away. A third problem was the reference to "Bjarni and Leif in company." None of the sagas mentions a voyage undertaken by these two seamen jointly; Bjarni's alleged landfall in Vinland preceded Leif's alleged landfall by some fifteen years.

Also, the map bore no date. The name of the person responsible for it was unknown. Finally, there was its perplexing physical association in a nineteenth-century binding, with the manuscript entitled "Incipit Historia Tartarorum." Why should this Tartar Relation, describing in Latin the land of the Mongols in Asia, be bound together with a map of the world with inscriptions about Norse voyages to a place called Vinland?

Apparently the only possible way to avoid having to cata-logue the map simply as an ancient curio with no historical anchorage was to assign a date to the Tartar Relation and then prove that map and manuscript had snuggled in the same bind-ing since their inception. The nineteenth-century rebinding was of course an obstacle to this, as were the Tartar Relation's lack of date or antecedent: like the map, its father and mother were unknown, there were no existing documents of which it was a copy. A few words in the Tartar Relation corresponded roughly with words on the map, designating places in Asia, of course, not America.

So, if the map could be proven to have been bound orig-inally with the 32-page Tartar Relation, if the latter could be assigned a date, if this date were earlier than 1492, and if people could be persuaded to accept that the Vinland on the map was a representation of North America, then this pyramid of ifs would show that Christopher Columbus was not the discoverer of America. But how was Laurence Witten to demonstrate that the map and the Tartar Relation were chronological twins? He was confronted with five difficulties.

Those difficulties were five worms.

Some old books are not only read by bookworms, they are inhabited by them. The inhabiting bookworms are the original species, as distinguished from the modern ones, the human beings who prefer a smooth leather volume to a cocktail glass, literature to limelight and bibliography to bibulousness. We are here concerned only with the original species, the worm that breakfasts, lunches and dines on, in and through books. Both kinds of bookworm may be concerned with the taste of a book, but with differing connotations. At any rate, four of the crawl-ers had found the Vinland Map, we may suppose, to be ade-quately tasty, because four holes in each of its two folds told the story of four worms who had eaten their way through its geography. If the Tartar Relation also had four wormholes which corresponded to the holes in the map this would indicate that the map and the Tartar Relation went together, the first step on the tortuous road leading to the dethronement of Columbus. But the worms were not cooperative: the Tartar Relation had only one wormhole, and it did not match up with any of the wormholes in the Vinland Map. Laurence Witten was baffled. He felt that the map might be a treasure in his hand, but without some proof of its association with another and indubitably pre-Columbian document, it became merely an interesting, enigmatic, but not especially valuable relic of unknown date.

However, soon after Witten's purchase, an extraordinary coincidence seems to have taken place. In 1958 Dr. Thomas Marston, Curator of Medieval and Renaissance Literature at the Yale University Library, purchased from a British shop a manuscript consisting of a portion of a work entitled Speculum Historiale (Mirror of History), written by a Franciscan monk, Father Vincent of Beauvais. The Speculum Historiale in its entirety was an encyclopedia telling the story of the world from Creation up to 1255, and was made up of 32 books. The manuscript purchased by Dr. Marston consisted only of four books, 21 to 24, although it had originally begun with book 20. It was written on 239 leaves or 478 pages, in its original (presumably) fifteenth-century binding. About 65 sheets or 130 pages, containing the missing book 20 and the table of contents for book 21, had disappeared from the front of the volume.

The Speculum Historiale in its entirety existed in various manuscripts, with no standard number of bound volumes to encompass its 32 books. The finding of a single portion by Dr. Marston, inscribed as being the third part (of a multi-volume copying), hardly constituted a bibliographic find of the first order. (So as to avoid confusion between the Speculum Historiale in its entirety and the single portion of it in the Yale Library, I will from now on refer to the latter manuscript as the Yale Speculum.) Nor, on the face of it, would Dr. Marston's purchase have any place in the authentication of the Vinland Map, for this Yale Speculum dealt only with world history running from A.D. 411 to 801, nearly two centuries before the first alleged Norse landings in America (and some four and a half centuries before the Carpini expedition to the Mongols treated in the Tartar Relation). The whereabouts of the other volumes of Yale's particular manuscript were unknown, and remain so, but their contents are well known to scholars from other hand-copied or printed editions which have survived in full.

On the back of the Vinland Map there appeared a laconic notation in Latin, which the Yale University Press translates as follows: "Delineation of the first part, the second part (and) the third part of the Speculum." Could Dr. Marston's acquisition be the one edition of the Speculum Historiale, out of all of the many that had been copied or printed through the centuries, that this strange map was created to illustrate, and with which this map had originally been bound? The possibility naturally intrigued both Witten and Marston, but their efforts to locate the missing parts of the Speculum proved fruitless, and whatever light they might have shed on the mystery at hand remains unemitted.

Even without this absent evidence speculation quickly jelled into certainty in their minds. When Dr. Marston showed Witten the manuscript he had bought, Witten asked if he could take it home and study it in connection with the map and the Tartar Relation. Late that night Witten telephoned Marston and exclaimed that the mystery had been solved. For Witten the pieces of the jigsaw puzzle had been put together, the enigma had melted away. Witten excitedly declared to Dr. Marston that the Speculum volume he had just examined was the connecting link between the map and the Tartar Relation. He said that the three had been bound together in the fifteenth-century binding which now contained only the truncated third part of the Speculum. With an eclat worthy of Sherlock Holmes cracking a seemingly impossible case, the dealer in old books had found a "home" for his map, had bridged the gap which would lead to dating the chart and, eventually, to the extraordinary announcement that would rock the pedestal of Columbus.

And what was the clue that impelled Witten to make so precipitate a telephone call of revelation?

Worms.

Worms that had eaten holes in the Vinland Map, the Tartar Relation and the Speculum Historiale. Holes, which Witten told Dr. Marston, matched, proving that the three entities had once been binding-mates. The wormtracks indicated, theorized

Witten, that the map had come first, the Speculum (the meat of this encyclopedic sandwich) in the middle, and the Tartar Relation last. The three components had, he said, at some unspecified time in the dim past, become separated, with the Speculum permitted to remain in its original fifteenth-century binding (which had been repaired in modern times) and the two slices of bread of the sandwich (the map and the Tartar manuscript) rebound by themselves in the nineteenth century. And now, after untold years apart, the trio of parts had come together again in one place. Surely the Sun of Happy Coincidence shone brightly in New Haven in 1958!

Witten's brief inspection of the Yale Speculum had also convinced him that the paper and handwriting of his and Dr. Marston's acquisitions were identical. Eventually many authorities were to become interested in these and other phases of the investigation into the genuineness and significance of the map, some of these authorities at the behest of the Yale Library, others independently. Not all of them, as we shall see, supported the thesis adumbrated by Witten, accepted by Yale's Library, set forth in an imposing book, and trumpeted to the world on the eve of Columbus Day, 1965, by the University's News Bureau. But for the time being, there was the aura of discovery at New Haven, the academic feverishness that once caused Archimedes to leap out of his bathtub, shout "Eureka!" and announce that he had just discovered specific gravity or something. Convinced of the specific gravity of their own findings, convinced that map and manuscripts had been created together and that the manuscripts preceded Columbus' voyage by about fifty years, Witten and Marston were preparing to drop their historical bombshell.

But before this could be done there was the problem of ownership. Both map and Speculum were in private hands (the map and Tartar Relation now technically owned by Mrs. Witten). It was important to bring the three musketeers under a single ownership, and that, preferably, of a scholarly institution. Thereupon, Dr. Marston gave his Speculum manuscript to Mrs. Witten, hoping, as he writes in *The Vinland Map and the Tartar Relation* (p. 4), "that this generosity would give the Yale

Library some element of control over the disposition of the map in the event that Mrs. Witten should decide to sell it."

Later the map and its two companions were sold to the Yale Library, the transaction made possible by an unnamed donor, and for an unrevealed price, estimates ranging from more than a quarter of a million dollars to nearly a million. And for those without the pocket money to buy the original, the Yale University Press prepared its weighty tome, four pounds weighty, *The Vinland Map and the Tartar Relation* (which I will refer to hereafter as the Vinland-Tartar book). Published (naturally) on Columbus Day, 1965, this book, besides reproductions of the map and the story of the Mongols and a translation of the latter, contains articles by three of the scholars who worked on the identification of the map: Dr. Thomas E. Marston, George D. Painter, Assistant Keeper of Printed Books in the British Museum, and R. A. Skelton, Superintendent of the Map Room of the British Museum.

And so we end the recent history of the Vinland Map on the eve of Columbus Day, 1965, with the map proud and ready to receive the first of its public visitors in the Beinecke Library on the morrow, the Vinland-Tartar book arriving hopefully on the shelves of booksellers, the editors of the nation's newspapers examining the febrile press release from Yale and finding its brashness and gimmickry worthy of a holiday feature story. And Columbus, sailing on in the hearts and minds of millions preparing to celebrate again the anniversary of his unfoldment of a New World . . . Columbus, sailing on, unaware of the torpedo scudding towards him.

Chapter 3

OUT OF THE BLUE

I do not question the right of the Yale University Press to unfurl a map and claim, through its publicity organ, that it proves Columbus did not discover America. This is academic freedom, freedom of the press and freedom of expression. But the Yale University Press is a responsible organization, bearing the name of one of the world's most honored seats of learning. Surely, before blaring out a crescendo of publicity so patently composed to drum up sales for its map with its accompanying book, while drumming Columbus out of his rightful place in history, the Yale Press should have taken another long, critical look at the object of all its fanfare. If they had done this, their gaze would have been greeted by a map as devoid of genealogical antecedents as a strange fish hauled out of the middle of the ocean on a moonless night and disappearing before daylight returns.

When the status quo is challenged, when the books of accepted fact are to be rewritten, the burden of proof falls always on the challenger, the rewriter. And when he offers his evidence in proof, be it a document or a dinosaur bone, a manuscript or a mummy, he is under a moral obligation to withhold nothing he may know about it, to say where and how and from whom it was obtained. The experts in the various disciplines whose task it is to test each new hopeful addition to the world's knowledge cannot be any more accurate than the amount of information they receive allows them to be.

The Vinland Map is offered. On the basis of it we are to

think about certain things a little differently than we thought before. Well and good, but before we change our thinking: where did the map come from? That is the first question I put when I first learned about the map.

If someone offered to wager that your home town was in the middle of the Gobi Desert, and then produced as proof a map showing your home town right in the middle, indeed, of the Gobi Desert, you would automatically ask: Where did you get that map? If someone deigned to add to your fund of knowledge by presenting you with an inscribed map, whose inscriptions showed Washington crossing not the Delaware but the Amazon and Lincoln born not in Kentucky but in Maine, again you would ask: Where did you get that map? And if the Yale University Press presents us with a map purporting to prove that Columbus did not discover America, shouldn't we ask: Where did you get that map?

On October 11, 1965, a staff member of the United Press International, Pittsburgh office, telephoned to ask if I had any comment to make on a "Vinland Map" "newly" discovered, which, according to a release they had received, showed that Columbus had not discovered America. The UPI called me because the staff knew of my lifelong participation in Italian-American affairs and of my Italian background.

I had made a particular study of Columbus' first voyage. This had culminated in my pilgrimage to San Salvador on Columbus Day, 1957, to plant an American flag and have a mass said at the spot where Columbus landed in 1492. I had also studied at the University of Rome and, while in Italy, had thoroughly researched the life of the Genoese navigator.

I asked the UPI reporter where the map had originated. He said he did not know and added that, according to dispatches received, the man who sold the map to Yale declined to state where he got it or from whom he obtained it. I gave the UPI a statement after seeing the map and it was published.

As a member and trustee of the Italian Historical Society of America, New York City, I decided to examine the original map and did so in the Beinecke Rare Book and Manuscript Library in New Haven. After studying the map, the Tartar Re-

lation and the Yale Speculum for most of a day, I walked over
to the antiquarian bookshop of Laurence Witten two or three
blocks away.

Although Mr. Witten had been voluble about the wormholes in the map and their alleged coincidence with wormholes
in the Speculum, he had been silent as a sphinx about his source
for the map. I decided to put a direct question to this man who
held the key to the map's past. I hoped he would produce this
key which would unlock the mystery of the map's antecedents. I
was obliged to leave without seeing him because he was occupied at the time with a customer. A few days later, however,
telephoning him from Philadelphia (where our Court was in
session), I received the greatest cordiality from him. He expressed regret that he had not been able to confer with me
while I was in his shop. I thanked him for his courtesies and
said: "I'm sorry we didn't have an opportunity to talk last Friday. I wouldn't have taken much of your time because I really
wanted to ask only one question."

"And what was that question?"

"I wanted to ask you where you got the Vinland Map."

"Well, in that case it wouldn't have done you any good to
wait because I wouldn't have answered your question."

"Why?"

"Because I wouldn't."

"Will you answer it now?"

"No, I will not answer it now."

"I'm sorry, Mr. Witten, and I don't want to seem to impor-
tune you, but it appears to me that it should be easy to say in a
very few words just where you got the Vinland Map."

"No, I gave an oath never to disclose where I got the map."

"To whom did you give such an oath?"

"To the person from whom I bought the map."

My consolation for this fruitless exchange was that the
members of the press had been unable to get any more from
Mr. Witten than I. Nevertheless, in balancing the right of the
American public, and the world's, to be given all the information necessary to make up its mind when asked to change its
thinking on so important a matter, as against the right of Mr.

Witten to remain secretive and make it impossible for scholars adequately to trace and verify the map's origin, I cannot help feeling regret that Witten made the choice of secrecy.

If I wished to purchase a book, a map, a manuscript, a document of any kind, which I hoped to exhibit to the world as an important historical discovery if it proved authentic, and the man proposing to sell it to me insisted on complete secrecy surrounding the transaction, I would, at the least, be alerted.

I would not withhold from the brave Norsemen their proper credit for discovering Greenland just because someone presented a crude map with an inscription next to Greenland, "Cleopatra barged in here," if the map came with no verifiable pedigree; nor do I intend displacing Christopher Columbus in my mind's pantheon as the discoverer of America on the basis of a map of dubious face and no pedigree.

It is hard to imagine that a man of Laurence Witten's obvious intelligence and erudition (he is a graduate of Yale) and business acumen (as demonstrated by his sale of the map to Yale) could either fail to realize his duty to the public or purchase a document under stultifying conditions. Perhaps the explanation for Witten's silence is suggested by a statement of his appearing in the New York *Herald Tribune,* October 11, 1965. Asked for the name of the person who sold him the map, Witten replied: "All I can say is that the European collector may be very cross when he finds out what he sold."

Several weeks later I returned to New Haven to study once more, and at length, with microscope and ruler, the Vinland Map and its manuscript companions at the Beinecke Library. I was accompanied by Philip Lombardo, a lawyer friend of mine from New York City, and John Gaudiosi, a professional photographer. Alexander O. Vietor, Curator of Maps of the Yale University Library, graciously allowed Mr. Gaudiosi to take as many pictures as he wished of the Vinland Map and the manuscripts. With Mr. Lombardo and Mr. Gaudiosi, I then again visited Mr. Witten's place of business. It was certainly an arresting looking shop, crowded with all kinds of ancient manuscripts, parchments, maps and other incunabula, most conspicuous among them an enlargement of the Vinland Map that struck the eye as soon as one entered the place. Tacked to the wall were front pages of newspapers whose headlines proclaimed the results of Witten's salesmanship. There was the home town paper, the New Haven *Journal-Courier* of October 11, asserting YALE MAP JARS COLUMBUS CLAIM; and the New York *Daily News* (BELIEVE COLUMBUS DISCOVERED AMERICA? YALE SAYS HE DIDN'T); and the New York *Herald Tribune* (VIKING DID BEAT COLUMBUS).

On this visit Witten was free to see us. He received us cordially and talked quite freely about his work and even the Vinland Map, although refusing to be drawn into any discussion having to do with the origin of the map. He discussed manuscripts he had handled, showed us an ancient Florentine manuscript, falling to pieces, about Caesar, and he used this property to illustrate his theory as to what might have happened to the Yale Speculum.

I repeated the question I had put to him over the telephone and received the same response, or rather lack of response. He would not reveal the name of the person who had sold the map to him. I thought he might bridle at my next question: "Well, if you won't tell us how and where you secured the map, perhaps you will tell us how and when the man you secured the map from, secured the map." Witten seemed quite undisturbed as he answered:

"Well, I will tell you frankly that I asked the owner of the map that very question and he replied that he didn't know where the map had come from."

During our conversation, Mr. Witten remarked that at the time he obtained the map he had wondered why the owner sold it, when it appeared, to Witten, such an exceedingly valuable property. "It could be that the owner thought the map was a fake and, therefore, was willing to get rid of it." He quickly added "Of course I know it isn't a fake."

As we walked down York Street afterwards, passing the ivy-curtained buildings of the University, I remarked to my friends that I could not understand why the Yale Library officials did not question Witten with regard to the origin of the map. "Perhaps they did," suggested Lombardo, "but got no satisfactory response."

But if the Yale officials did ask Witten about this matter and he refused to divulge his source, it seems to me that they should have said something like: "Mr. Witten, we cannot afford to display in our library a document so potentially disruptive of history as we know it, we cannot afford to bolster the acceptance of so potentially controversial a document with the name and reputation of our University, unless we are in a position to reveal all that can be learned about the past life of this document."

Or if the Yale officials did ask Witten, and he answered them fully, then the moral obligation to provide the map with its pedigree falls squarely on the shoulders of these officials.

As late as February, 1966, according to the London *Sunday Times*, Witten said that the map could not be traced back past the owner from whom he bought it. "I assure you," he said, "that aspect is a blind alley."

We face here the astonishing spectacle of all the scholarly fraternity, all the world's experts on ancient maps and manuscripts, and medieval and Renaissance literature and cartography, being asked to accept, merely on Laurence Witten's unadorned say-so, that tracing the map's history is impossible. With all due respect for the astuteness and professional knowledge of Laurence Witten, how can he possibly know, as fact, that if his source for the map were revealed, the information would not provide a single clue for a single expert to take up the scent? Give the experts a crack at the case! Mr. Witten's "blind alley" may be someone else's highway to truth, and the toll needed for driving on this highway may be simply to know where the map was when Witten came across it.

Suppose a dealer in rare books suddenly announced that he had discovered a manuscript of a lost play by Shakespeare, in the author's own hand. And suppose that attempts to authenticate it on technical grounds—paper, ink, writing, etc.—were promising but inconclusive, and that a number of Shakespearean authorities rejected it out of hand, judging it as not by the

Bard on grounds of literary style. Would it not then be a matter of the utmost urgency, before the play be added to the Shakespeare canon, for its discoverer to say where he found it? Could the world be expected to accept as genuine the most startling literary find of all time without even the chance to reconstruct its history, simply because its discoverer chose silence?

Is this a fair analogy to the case of the Vinland Map? I quote from the foreword (p. v) by Alexander O. Vietor, Curator of Maps at the Yale University Library, to the Vinland-Tartar book. Speaking of the map and the Tartar Relation, he says that lacking a continuous history of their past, it cannot be categorically proven "that they are not counterfeit."

Out of the blue comes the Vinland Map. Or, at any rate, from an anonymous European source who "may be very cross when he finds out what he sold."

And might not the Yale Library, someday, be very cross when it finds out what it bought?

Chapter 4

"BOAT LEAVING FOR SATANAXES . . ."

The Vinland Map is claimed by its supporters to be the oldest existing chart of any part of the American continents. It is supposed to be based on the recorded observations—nowhere to be found today and nowhere mentioned as ever existing—of the Norse mariners whose exploits, real and imagined, are related in the sagas.

Assuming, as the map's supporters are forced to, that some long-since-vanished record containing a map or verbal description of "Vinland" was available to the drawer of the Vinland Map—or to the drawer of some putative map from which the Vinland Map was copied—what credit can be awarded to the observational powers of the compiler of such a record? Can the most charitable examiner see North America in "Vinland"?

No Vinland-devotee has made the suggestion, to my knowledge, that the geographical monstrosity on the map represents anything more than the northeastern corner of our continent, yet it is shown as an island. Lest any of those who have identified Vinland with Newfoundland say it is merely that island that is represented, it should be pointed out that Vinland on the map is far larger than Greenland or Great Britain, and its outline resembles Newfoundland no more than any other place on the globe. Short of claiming, then, that the Viking mariners succeeded in circumnavigating the entire North and South American land mass, modestly keeping it secret except from the maker of the Vinland Map, the map's apologists are in the position of having to explain why the northeastern sector of North

America should be shown as an island. The Viking discoverers, they might say, mapped or described the Atlantic coastline somewhere between Labrador and New England, and merely guessed that this was part of an island. Some island!

Guesses do not constitute geography. Nor, as a supposed representation of the northeastern coastline of North America, is the Vinland blob anything less than an affront. The lake in the northern portion of the blob, with a river connecting it with the ocean, *may*, we are told, represent Hudson Bay and Hudson Strait; the narrow inlet to the south *may* be the estuary of the St. Lawrence. On the other hand, they *may* be, respectively, the St. Lawrence and the Hudson. What it amounts to, I fear, is that once you decide arbitrarily what the mapmaker was trying to show, you just go ahead and make your own identification.

Unless those claiming historical significance for the Vinland Map get together and decide, among themselves, just where Vinland was (we shall meet some of their divergent theories later) and hence exactly what place it is that the map depicts, how can they assert that the map is a geographical representation of anything?

How authentic a document can it be?

During my thirty-four years as a judge I have had to pass on the authenticity of thousands of documents. My judicial experience leads me to conclude that no court in a civilized country would accept as genuine the Vinland Map on the basis of the shaky, internally inconsistent proofs offered by the authors of the Vinland-Tartar book. It is even admitted by Mr. Vietor, in his foreword to the book (p. vi), while reaffirming on behalf of Yale's team the authenticity of the map "without reservation," that the case for this authenticity is "in part circumstantial" and falls short of "legal proof."

Let us look briefly at a few of the criteria for legal proof and see if there is anything about them contrary to good common sense. Let us then ask ourselves, since we are asked to accept the Vinland Map as a genuine document of the utmost importance in the history of mankind, whether this map may be considered uniquely exempt from fulfilling the criteria of legal proof.

Some people may be convinced of the authenticity of the Vinland Map simply because it looks so ancient and crude, but appearance of age can be deceiving. No chemical tests have been carried out, at this writing, to determine the age of ink or parchment, but the secrecy surrounding the map's purchase and consequent lack of evidence as to its whereabouts over the centuries present a formidable obstacle to the usefulness of any such tests. J. Newton Baker says, in his monumental "Law of Disputed and Forged Documents" (Charlottesville, Va.: The Michie Co., 1955):

> "The determination of the exact age of ink writing is difficult and is only speculation in most instances unless it is based on circumstantial evidence. Exposure to light, moisture and varied atmospheric conditions affects the condition and durability of ink . . . When an attempt is made to determine or testify as to the age of written instruments without knowing the circumstances of the writing or the composition of the ink, the probability of reaching an accurate opinion of the age of the writing is very remote in the face of the possibilities of modern chemistry." (Sec. 254)

Was the Vinland Map, at the time of its modern rediscovery, in some place where it would be natural to find a genuine document of such a nature? "A forger can usually not secure the placing of the document in such a custody; and hence the naturalness of its custody, being relevant circumstantially, is required in combination with the document's age." ("Wigmore on Evidence," Boston: Little Brown & Co., 1940, sec. 2139)

What do we know of the naturalness of the custody of the Vinland Map? Nothing. Albert S. Osborn in his work "Questioned Documents" points out: "The unexplained mystery surrounding the custody of a surprising document also may be the basis for grave suspicion. If it is not genuine, a document must be directly assailed and its weaknesses and shortcomings exposed . . . The actual age of a document is ascertained by a study of all the means by which it was produced and the actual conditions under which it was kept. All the external evidence bearing on the question should be thoroughly investigated." (Albany, N.Y.: Wm. Boyd Printing Co., 1910, pp. 569–70)

It is impossible to examine the "external evidence bearing on the question" when we do not know where the Vinland Map was obtained, nor from whom, nor where the previous owner had it nor where he had obtained it, and so forth. Mr. Osborn comments: "The collector must be warned to be constantly on his guard against forgeries. There are great quantities of spurious specimens in circulation. The French (although their laws are severe against all frauds) are wonderfully clever in manufacturing autographs. This probably accounts for the number of interesting French documents of the great characters of the last century, from Louis XIV to Napoleon, always on sale at very moderate prices." (p. 571)

Another requirement of the law, and of common sense, is that an aged controverted document "must exhibit an honest face; otherwise it is not such an ancient document that its countenance will pass muster. Age will not sanctify ear-marks of fraud." (Wigmore, sec. 2140)

The countenance of the Vinland Map bears birthmarks of self-invalidation. In the middle of its Atlantic Ocean appear two great islands, irregularly rectangular in shape with the longer axis north-south. Between them is the legend "Magnae Insulae Beati Brandani Branziliae dictae." The combined area of these two land masses is about equal to that of the British Isles. They are, and were in 1440, non-existent.

If the Vinland Map was drawn in 1440, and the quality of its author's geographical sophistication is epitomized by his apparent belief in the existence in mid-Atlantic of islands the size of Great Britain and Ireland, why are we meekly to accept, as a "cartographic representation" (Vinland-Tartar, p. v) of anything, his Vinland?

During the initial furore over Yale's extravagant press release, the New York *World-Telegram* printed a cartoon by

Berry showing a monk at a desk, pen in hand, telling a brother monk: "I think I'll throw in a couple of extra islands on this map, just for laughs."

In attempting to explain away the two mid-Atlantic embarrassments, the editors of the Vinland-Tartar book state that the drawer of the map was merely a copyist, that other maps before his had carried these imaginary islands with the names Satanaxes and Antillia. But then, from where did he copy Vinland if he was merely a copyist? It had not appeared on any previous map. Perhaps it was added later—much later—or perhaps our scribe was simply fishing islands out of the sea of imagination, "just for laughs," and hooked Satanaxes and Antillia from the lore of medieval cartography and Vinland from the lore of Norse adventure.

This, then, is what Mr. Vietor, in the Vinland-Tartar book (p. v) introduces as "the earliest known and indisputable cartographic representation of any part of the Americas." It is not surprising, in view of the realities, as will appear herein, that many well qualified persons have come forward to dispute the "indisputable." Long before publication of the book, according to the London *Sunday Times* in its March 6, 1966 article, Eva Taylor, Professor Emeritus of Geography at the University of London, informed the members of the commission preparing Yale's book that, in her opinion, the map could not be of the fifteenth century. It is her contention that the map is a twentieth-century hybrid, different elements deriving from different modern publications, including modern facsimiles of old maps. An error on the Vinland Map in the relative positions of Iceland, the Faroe and Shetland Islands and Ireland is identical with one in the 1569 world map of Mercator, and its scale is identical with that of a twentieth-century reproduction of the Mercator. Professor Taylor is cited, in the *Times* article, as "possibly the world's most distinguished authority on medieval cartography."

Mr. G. R. Crone, in the February, 1966 *Encounter* article previously quoted, states: "The copyist's treatment of his world model debars him from serious consideration as a cosmographer

or cartographer. Further, his abilities thus revealed lend no
support whatever to the authenticity of the Vinland section; in
fact, it is left open to very serious doubt."

It is hardly disputable that if land the size of Vinland, as
depicted on the Vinland Map, had been discovered prior to
1440, it would have been an event of sufficient importance to
galvanize the attention of the great cartographers of the eras
immediately preceding and following that decade. But there
was not the slightest cognizance of any such western land in the
world maps produced by such famous mapmakers as Giovanni
da Carignano, Petrus Vesconte, Marco and Francesco Pizzigano
and Fra Mauro, whose works extended from 1310 to 1459. The
world map in the Laurentian ("Medici") sea atlas (1351),
showed only blankness where now the Vinland Map flaunts an
enormous land mass supposedly settled by the year 1117. The
1436 world map of the illustrious Andrea Bianco of Venice, regarded as one of the most authoritative maps of that era and
suggested by the editors of the Vinland-Tartar book as deriving
from the same primary source as the Vinland Map, carries no
hint of great lands to the west.

It is strange enough that Vinland does not appear on any
known chart predating the parchment in Yale's Library, particularly since the settlement it commemorates is supposed to have
taken place well over three centuries prior to 1440. But an even
more annihilating blow to the pretensions of the Vinland Map
as a historical document is the failure of Vinland to appear on
maps *after* 1440! Following hundreds of years in cartographic
limbo, our island rises from the sea in 1440, to bask in the sunshine for one day like the town of Brigadoon, and then sinks
under the brine again . . . not to reappear until 1590. For it
was about that year, a century after Columbus, that a chart-
maker first attached the names of the Vikings' landfalls from the
saga tales to the land across the Atlantic, now already discovered
and explored by Columbus, Cabot, Verrazano and others. On
the map of the North Atlantic of that date by Sigurdur Stefansson (of which there exists only a 1670 copy), a continental
mass, of which Greenland is shown as a peninsula, is marked
with the place names Helleland, Markland, Skraelinge Land,

and Promontorium Winlandiae. These first three names were taken from the sagas, the fourth was invented by Stefansson.

Map making can be said to have become a science with the Greeks, at least as far back as the sixth century B.C. By the time of Aristotle, in the fourth century B.C., the idea of a spherical earth was already firmly established. This science of cartography reached an early apotheosis in the magnificent work of Claudius Ptolemy of Alexandria about 150 A.D. His charts still influenced the geographers of the fifteenth century. It is very difficult to believe that the sketcher of the Vinland Map—so incompetent compared even to Ptolemy thirteen centuries earlier—had a knowledge of a "Vinland" that eluded all of his more able contemporaries, and the skill to draw an accurate Greenland.

It is asserted by the editors of the Vinland-Tartar book, as I will discuss at greater length later on, that the compiler of the Vinland Map accomplished his work at Basel, Switzerland, where ecclesiastics and sages from all parts of the world had gathered for a Church Council lasting from 1431 to 1449. And yet we are to believe that the depiction of huge new lands to the west, unknown to the drawers of the other world maps of the time, elicited no recorded notice or comment from the distinguished scholars who attended the Council. Strange.

In the Yale University Library, only a few feet away from the Vinland Map (as constantly guarded, by the way, as the gold at Fort Knox), there hangs the splendid and authentic world map drawn in 1489 by a German, then living in Italy, Henry Martellus Germanus. This Martellus map, six by four feet, was the subject of a special article by Alexander O. Vietor, Curator of Maps at the Yale University Library, in the Yale University Library Gazette of July, 1962 (five years after Mr. Witten brought the Vinland Map to New Haven). Mr. Vietor, in his article, describes the Martellus map as "the most important cartographical treasure ever received by Yale." Needless to say, the Martellus map does not show Vinland.

Nor does any Vinland appear on the world globe of Martin Behaim, displayed in Nuremberg in 1492, just before Columbus' first voyage. Behaim was an expert mapmaker who had lived for six years in Portugal and the Azores, where surely tidings of a continent across the Atlantic would have washed ashore if tidings there had been.

If we are to accept the outline of Vinland on the Vinland Map as representing actual geographic knowledge in the possession of the drawer of the map, or of some putative map from which he copied, let us examine some aspects of the state of the geographical knowledge of the known world of 1440 as reflected in the map.

The Vinland-Tartar book tells us that the map's compiler may have copied from Scandinavian sources or may have received information at the Basel Council from a visiting Scandinavian or may have been a Scandinavian himself, familiar at first hand with the data of the Norse voyages. In any one of these possibilities, we would have reason to expect that Scandinavia, of all places, would have adequate representation on the map. Yet we see the north-south peninsula that comprises Norway and Sweden on a modern map lying east-west on the Vinland Map, extending as far west as Great Britain. And where does our fifteenth-century cartographer place Sweden? South of the Baltic, in continental Europe, just west of Russia! Straight from the Norse's mouth.

The Danube River (which, the Vinland-Tartar book points out, is labelled with the name of the Don) is correctly shown flowing into the Black Sea, but it also flows through Poland into the Baltic, evidently confused by the mappist with the Oder or Vistula. The Isle of Wight is placed at the southeast corner of England instead of directly south. The Baltic is shown almost east-west, instead of generally north-south.

Rome, the intellectual, religious and cultural center of the world in 1440, is placed in the Alps on what is now the Swiss border! However indulgent we may be toward whoever was responsible for the cosmographical hash of the Vinland Map for the gross errors in the depiction of Asia and Africa, these parts of Europe were hardly *terrae incognitae,* especially at such a cosmopolitan gathering of sages and scholars as the Council at Basel.

Professor Eva Taylor is quoted in the London *Sunday Times* article of March 6, 1966, as pointing out: "The gross misplacing of Crete, the faulty Aegean Sea, and the absence of the Sea of Marmora are strange features on a map purporting to be of the mid-fifteenth century, when extremely accurate charts of the Mediterranean Sea were available."

". . . a forger often betrays himself by not knowing quite enough about the field in which he is working," she adds.

Surely the most delicious solecism on the Vinland Map is the southern coastline of its drastically truncated version of Africa. G. R. Crone, in his *Encounter* review, reveals that this corresponds with a chance fold in the Bianco world map from which he feels strongly that the Vinland Map was derived (except for Vinland itself, of course). Mistaking an accidental fold for a coastline is equivalent to a musician's playing the flyspecks along with the notes.

Our school children today are being taught something called "the new mathematics." If on Columbus Day, 1965, there was born "the new history," or history by press release and wormy map, are we now to laud the anonymous scribe who drew the Vinland Map for the creation of "the new geography"?

"Boat leaving for Satanaxes and Antillia, with stopover at Vinland . . ."

Chapter 5

FROZEN CUSTODY

There are four ways to produce a map. One is to visit the place you are going to map and draw what you see, or, if you are more sophisticated, draw what your instruments "see." Another method is to draw your map from data submitted by competent surveyors, navigators, explorers. A third way is to copy it from another map; and the fourth way is to make it up out of your head.

No one contends or even suggests that the Vinland Map's artist ever visited the land he calls Vinland on his map.

If Vinland was based on the competent data of others, such data has not survived nor is there the slightest evidence that it ever existed. The Norse explorers were not known to make maps; the sailing directions and distances relating to their western landfalls given in the sagas are far too fragmentary and ambiguous to be of any use in helping a harassed mapmaker to eke out the far corners of his chart. And if it is argued that Vinland on the map is based on some now-lost data compiled by pre-Columbian explorers, to what place on earth can such data refer? What looks like this Vinland?

Since the first two methods of making a map cannot be applied to the case of the Vinland Map, and since for obvious reasons they wish to avoid any suggestion of the fourth, the editors of the Vinland-Tartar book bank heavily on the third way: to copy from another map. But where is this map? or maps? The Anglo-American team of experts who have "authenticated" the

Vinland Map have the burden of demonstrating that their "baby" had a mother. While offering a rather involved and speculative genealogy for the Old World portions of the map, classifying it with the 1436 Bianco map for general type, they admit they are stumped when it comes to suggesting a prototype for the Vinland-Greenland portion of the map. And it's that northwest corner that hit the headlines and cost Yale's donor a fortune.

The libraries and monasteries and other repositories of ancient records, all over the world, have constantly been ransacked by antiquarians, yet no pre-Columbian map of the Western Hemisphere has reared its head. In a succinct elucidation of the dilemma set forth in the Vinland-Tartar book (p. 178) by Mr. Skelton, he admits that determining the source for the map is a purely hypothetical exercise, since no supporting document exists: research on the map leads to a dead end. But even if a pre-Vinland-Map map were to show up, what guarantee of authenticity would this lend? It would only indicate that the Vinland Map drawer was not the first to foist a cartographic chimera, a geographic supposition based on legend and not evidence, upon a scholarly fraternity apparently too unimpressed to take notice.

G. R. Crone, Librarian and Map Curator of the Royal Geographical Society, London, in the previously cited *Encounter* review of the Vinland-Tartar book, concludes his analysis of the Vinland Map with the opinion that the only basic source for it was the 1436 Andrea Bianco world map, and that the depiction of Vinland "possibly derives in part from a reading of the (Norse) sagas . . ." From his observation that a fold in Bianco's original was mistaken by the Vinland Map copyist for the southern coast of Africa, Crone concludes that it was this original, in Venice since its creation, that was the model for the Old World portions. "Probably post-Columbian" is his negative verdict on the Vinland Map.

Now for the loudest shot in Yale's armamentarium.

Not many viewers are likely to be impressed by the resemblance to North America of the map's Vinland—with its "Hudson Bay" and dire strait in the north, and "St. Lawrence River"

—rapids pulled out of a hat—in the south. But, aha! Look at Greenland!

One can only agree with the map's advocates that the outline of Greenland is startlingly accurate. Many a schoolchild could identify it properly at first glance, so closely does it conform to the shape of Greenland on a modern map. In fact, school children with good marks in geography would be more likely to recognize Greenland on the map than, for instance, England, or Italy with its toe missing. Far and away the greatest enigma shrouding the Vinland Map is the discrepancy between the amazingly true contours of Greenland and the rough, slipshod portrayal of centers of European civilization and population.

If the map is genuine, if it was indeed drawn in its entirety around 1440, it seems to me that it should have been proclaimed as the Greenland Map, not the Vinland Map. No conclusion can fairly be drawn from the Vinland ogre that it "proves" a Norse discovery of North America, but it is difficult to avoid jumping to fantastic conclusions about Greenland . . . if the map is genuine. Maybe the emphasis in the publicity is occasioned by the fact that there are more bookstores in "Vinland" than in Greenland.

How well was Greenland known to cartographers prior to modern times? The Vinland-Tartar book itself helps answer this question by reproducing various maps of the North Atlantic drawn subsequent to 1440. Here is how the world's largest island was known: the Martellus map of 1480 shows Greenland as a peninsula from Europe extending almost as far west as Ireland; the map of John Ruysch of 1508 portrays it as a peninsula stemming from Asia; the Zeno map of the North Atlantic of 1558 shows Greenland as a part of Europe; Mercator's world map of 1569 makes of it an extension of a mythical Arctic land; the Stefansson map of 1590 has Greenland a peninsula projecting from North America; the Hans Poulson Resen map of 1605 does likewise; and the Thorlaksson map of 1606 leaves its northern extent to the imagination but brings its eastern extremity very close to Scandinavia. On not one of these maps does Greenland assume the form it has on the Vinland Map of (supposedly) 1440. What genius caused the Vinland Map copy-ist or his model to learn by 1440 what it took the rest of human-ity more than another 400 years to find out?

The *Encyclopaedia Britannica,* in its article on Greenland, states that it was not until 1822 that there was made "the first fairly trustworthy map of the coast between 69 and 75 deg. N." The German Koldewey expedition reached 77 deg. N. (Cape Bismarck) in 1870; it was not until 1906–08 that the Danish Erichsen-Koch expedition explored the rest of the northern east coast. E. Mikkelsen mapped this region in 1909–12.

To offer the Vinland Map's Greenland as the end product of Viking exploration is to make the gratuitous assumption that the Norse voyagers, against any evidence in the very sagas them-selves or any other source, succeeded in circumnavigating Green-land in their crude open boats the better part of a millennium before anyone else. This would entail approaching to nearly five degrees of the North Pole. Even accepting the theory that somewhat milder climatic conditions prevailed in Greenland in Norse days, and making full allowance for the splendid seafar-ing abilities and courage of the Viking sailors, such an astounding premise cannot be accepted on the strength of the Vinland Map. (Professor Taylor puts the northern limit to the Vikings' Greenland explorations at 76 degrees north latitude; Peary Land, the northern extension of Greenland, reaches about 83 degrees.)

If the medieval Vikings actually sailed completely around Greenland—establishing its island nature and accumulating sufficient data for a more accurate map to be made of it than contemporaries were making of Europe—then why and how did the makers, transmitters and preservers of the sagas of the Norse exploits, keep such a jealous custody over this feat that no word of it has come to us?

So surprising is the accuracy of the Greenland delineation, according to Franklin D. Scott in his New York *Herald Tribune* review of the Yale Press book, that "one looks again to make sure it wasn't added in the twentieth century."

Let us take the cue, if not the conclusion, for our windup of this discussion of the Greenland anomaly from R. A. Skelton, in his article in the Vinland-Tartar book (p. 197). Here the ugly idea of counterfeiting is brought up by Mr. Skelton, suggested to him by that amazingly correct Greenland, but nevertheless he lightly dismisses this thought in the map's favor.

Since the Vinland Map, as offered, is by an unknown copyist copying from an unknown map based on unknown records of unknown voyages, and since the Vinland Map itself was obtained from an unknown seller in an unknown place and has an unknown history, and since the map bears on its face the false nose of anachronism, I submit, as a more reasonable explanation than any given out by the Yale editors, that its over-enthusiastic Greenland and diffident Vinland were added subsequent to the creation of the rest of the map, which exhibited nothing further west than the imaginary islands of Satanaxes and Antillia.

If Greenland on the map is genuine, so's your Antillia!

Chapter 6

THE WORMS CRAWL IN,
THE WORMS CRAWL OUT

It is time now to turn our attention to Yale's center-ring act, the five performing worms.

It will be remembered that "the most exciting map discovery of the century" depended for the excitement it was to stir up, upon being associated physically with the Yale Speculum and Tartar Relation, manuscripts of assumed pre-Columbian date. This association was claimed to have been established by the matching of wormholes indicating that the Vinland Map had come first in the original binding, the Vincent of Beauvais Speculum Historiale second, and the Tartar Relation last.

Even if we were to accept Yale's thesis, it would not prove any more than that a particular piece of parchment was bound into a particular volume. Even the most talented trick-and-fancy-boring worm in the world, chomping synchronous figure-eights in map and Speculum, could not establish that no islands were added to the map *after* the worm had polished off his dessert. Which consideration may seem to make the whole brouhaha about the matching of the wormholes somewhat academic, but as long as such great store is set by the wormholes, as long as they are spotlighted as the clincher to Yale's chain of arguments, we will try to come to terms with them.

Almost all that has been written about the subject has indicated that the wormholes exactly matched, and that this was irrefutable proof of the original propinquity of the three documents. Buried here is the assumption that when a covey of worms with leonine appetites is turned loose on a yummy old book, they will fly in formation, as it were. In other words, they will chew exactly parallel courses and wind up, at the end of their odyssey (or Speculum) in the same relative positions and at precisely the same distance apart as when they began. If Yale's wormholes become the tunnels through which crawled the underminers of the belief that Columbus discovered America, and if their significance depends on the above implicit assumption, then it is important for us to see just exactly how the wormholes do match.

On page 109 of the Vinland-Tartar book is the account of how the original juxtaposition of the Vinland Map with the Yale Speculum was shown in Mr. Witten's demonstration. Three wormholes go through the two leaves of parchment of the map (it was folded in half, remember), matching precisely a set of holes in the first pages of the Speculum. A fourth wormhole is larger in the map's first sheet than in its second, and disappears altogether in the Speculum. This worm must have lost his appetite after chewing on the Vinland Map. I don't blame him.

He might also have lost his appetite if he could have foreseen how the feats of himself and his fellow trenchermen would be distorted in the molds of publicity. The campaign to put over the Vinland-Tartar book by brazenly discrediting Columbus built up a misleading picture. The average reader exposed to this publicity might well get the impression that wormholes went continuously through the Vinland Map, the thick Speculum manuscript, and the Tartar Relation. But after he paid his money for a copy of the Yale University Press book, he would learn that not one single wormhole penetrated all the way through any two of these documents, let alone all three. Further, as we shall see, the fact that the front part of the Speculum Historiale is missing means that the journey of the worms between map and manuscript is purely hypothetical, if indeed the same worms crawled out of the missing pages and into the pages of history-by-headline as crawled into them from the map.

It is noteworthy that the Vinland-Tartar book fails to describe in any detail the manner in which the worms allegedly knitted the three manuscripts together. If one examines the map, Yale Speculum and Tartar Relation in the Yale Library, as I did, one may get a clearer picture of how far short of their billing the performing worms fall.

The impression has been fostered that a large number of tallying wormholes punctured the three papers. Actually, there were five. And do these five coincide?

When I visited the Yale Library to conduct my examination, measurements were made, in the presence of Mr. Vietor, Dr. Marston, and Kenneth Nesheim, Assistant Librarian, of the distances from the edges of the pages to the wormholes in the map and in the Speculum.

For convenience I number the wormholes in the Vinland Map (all patched over with bits of vellum, by the way, at some unknown date) as follows:

No. 1: under Greenland

No. 2: west of Great Britain

No. 3: in Atlantic Ocean, close to the imaginary islands of Antillia and Satanaxes

No. 4: in Scandinavia

Wormhole No. 1 is the one that had no coincidence at all in the Speculum. Here are the distances of the others:

No. 2 hole

MAP	—from top of page to hole	89 mm.
SPECULUM	—from top of page to hole	88 mm.
MAP	—from left margin to hole	119 mm.
SPECULUM	—from left margin to hole	125 mm.

No. 3 hole

MAP	—from top of page to hole	119 mm.
SPECULUM	—from top of page to hole	120 mm.
MAP	—from left margin to hole	114 mm.
SPECULUM	—from left margin to hole	119 mm.

No. 4 hole

MAP	—from top of page to hole	45 mm.
SPECULUM	—from top of page to hole	46 mm.
MAP	—from left margin to hole	165 mm.
SPECULUM	—from left margin to hole	172 mm.

It will be noted that in every instance there was a discrepancy in the measurements between the holes in the map and the holes in the Speculum volume. Mr. Vietor pointed out that holes Nos. 2, 3 and 4 in the map appeared in the same relative positions as in the first page of the Speculum. In regard to the difference in the lineal measurements, he said that parchment crinkles whereas paper does not and that, therefore, the distances on the parchment map shortened over a period of years. But this does not suffice to explain why the differentiation in distance thus caused is not constant. As the above table of measurements makes clear, the discrepancy is not the same for any two holes. And if the very reasonable supposition is advanced that the worms simply did not travel in exactly parallel courses, then how can we be so sure that the wormholes in the Speculum are the termini of the same tracks begun in the map?

On p. 5 of the Vinland-Tartar book, Dr. Marston writes: "While the wormholes in VM do not match those of TR in number or position, those of VM do precisely match those at the beginning of Speculum, and the worming in TR precisely matches that in the final leaves of Speculum." We have seen that only three holes are adduced to bridge the gap between map and Speculum, and we have seen just how precise is their correspondence. Now what about "those of TR" or "the worming in TR"? How many are "those"?

One.

There is only one wormhole at the end of the Speculum volume and only one at the beginning of the Tartar Relation, a fact revealed only many pages later than the above quote, taken from the subchapter "Description of the Manuscript."

There has been no mention, in the ballyhoo about the wormholes, that there are sizeable differences in the depths to which they penetrate. Yet here is another point against the unreliability of postulating a physical association between the three documents on the basis of five worms. The first hole in the map, as will be recalled, does not enter the Speculum manuscript at all. Hole No. 2 penetrates to the depth of 3 leaves, Hole No. 3 to the depth of 12 leaves, and Hole No. 4 to the depth of 6 leaves. The only hole going the other way, from the Tartar Relation to the Speculum, penetrates the latter for 87 leaves. Adding these 87 leaves to the 12 leaves marking the penetration of the hungriest worm at the front of the volume, we get 99 wormed sheets . . . out of a total of 239. Thus there are 140 leaves in the center of the Yale Speculum with no worm tunnels at all.

The upshot of all this is that there is not a single worm track spanning the three works. Therefore, even accepting for the sake of argument that Yale has proven a physical association between map and Speculum, and one between Speculum and Tartar Relation, there is nothing to put the three together at the same time.

There is no way of dating the wormholes. How is one to be sure that two of the documents, or all three, were not brought together in the same binding long years after the supposed 1440 date of the copying of the Speculum, and *then* wormed? Even a single wormhole penetrating all three components of the sandwich—and, as we have seen, there isn't any—would indicate juxtaposition, yes, but *when?* Unless we can be sure that the worms began their safari in the years between 1440 and 1492, the proof that the map is pre-Columbian vanishes.

It is a shame that none of the five bookworms involved has left us his memoirs, so that we might know which of the books were together at what time. But none has, and it seems to me that guaranteeing the authenticity of a document, which informs the public that Christopher Columbus is henceforth no longer to be regarded as the discoverer of America, on the slitherings and squirmings of five worms, is a very slippery business indeed.

Before leaving this elusive subject of bookworms, I hope the reader will forgive me if I bring another 41 worms into the discussion. It is only fair that some brief notice should be taken of them, if the five worms of the manuscripts rate a whole chapter here. These are the 41 worms of the covers. The fifteenth-century binding of the Yale Speculum, put forth as the original binding of all three works, looks as if it had been blasted by a shotgun, front and back. There are some 17 wormholes in the front cover, about 24 in the back cover.

But not one of these holes penetrates through either cover to penetrate the front or rear of the manuscript. How did the four worms that ate their way through the Vinland Map get into it? Did they sneak in sideways, forgoing leathery appetizers in favor of parchment entree? How did the lone borer at the rear whose tastes encompassed a mission to the Mongols manage to sneak past two dozen of his fellows without leaving a hole in the cover himself?

The Yale team adduces other evidence to connect the Vinland Map with the two ancient manuscripts and give the map a pre-Columbian date of origin. As we shall see presently, this other evidence cannot be considered conclusive. It is the "precise" matching of the wormholes that is supposed to settle the issue beyond a shadow of a doubt. In view of this, perhaps it is not so surprising that the Vinland-Tartar editors and the book's publicists do not betray any awareness of the irony of using the labyrinthine twistings of five worms to repudiate the discovery of America by Columbus. Nor is there a word of appreciation in the impressive tome they have produced, so full of scholarly footnotes and references, for the yeoman service rendered their case by the worms. Nothing about the worms' habits, sense of direction, or appetite, nothing about their goals and dreams. Not even any speculation about whether Vinland and Greenland were on the map when the worms were passing through, and if they were, what the worms thought of them.

To those who attach more significance to the wormholes than I am able to, I leave this final disturbing thought: If a manuscript can be counterfeited, why not a wormhole? If the troops of Henry V could "imitate the action of the tiger," is it too much to believe that one might imitate the action of the worm?

I don't believe in forgery by wormhole myself.

Dinner for five, please, James.

Chapter 7

LEFTY COMES TO BAT

On October 11, 1965, the Yale University News Bureau announced in its publicity release that the Vinland Map "was drawn about 1440 A.D., probably by a monk in Basel, Switzerland." Neither his name nor his street address was given, but, even as it stands, the supposition suggests a brilliantly wrought piece of academic supersleuthing.

Actually, no intimation of Basel or any other point of origin is in the text of the Vincent of Beauvais work, the Vinland Map or the Tartar Relation, nor is there any internal clue in any of the three which might lead to a reasonable assignment of birthplace. But the more details, however hypothetical, that are used to buttress the basic contention that Columbus didn't discover America on the say-so of the map, the more impressed the public is likely to be by the veracity of the contention.

Someone in the Yale Press-Library enterprise, talking with a newspaper reporter, said that the unknown scribe was "possibly left-handed and possibly a secretary to a bigwig at the Roman Catholic Council." Suppose someone guessed that the unknown scribe was "possibly" right-handed and "possibly" nobody's secretary, who could prove he was wrong?

The attempt to flesh out the clanking skeleton of the scribe charged with the copying of the three documents, and give him vocation and location, in the absence of any information, can only be attributed to the need to cloak the Vinland Map's desperate lack of innate verisimilitude. No one knows whether the map's compiler was a monk, teacher, artist or left-handed lutenist. All that can be said with any degree of certainty is that he wasn't very attentive to his sources, as we shall see, and that, after copying the 1,450,000 words of the entire Speculum Historiale, he probably came down with writer's cramp.

The editors of the Vinland-Tartar book, seeking a date on which to hang their map, go into an extended discussion of a Church Council which was held in Basel, Switzerland, from 1431 to 1449. Dr. Marston says that this Council was important not only in the "conciliar movement," but also "in intellectual history." He relates that church notables with their staffs from all over the continent attended, and that the Council was "noted for introducing to Western European churchmen the Bible in Greek, and in spreading the ideas of the Italian humanists and their works to Northern Europeans." This impressive setting of the scene is followed by a question: "Where else could such a product as this be prepared, combining an East European account of a mission to the Mongols with a medieval historical text and a map of Northern European origin?" (p. 16)

"Basel certainly seems the most sensible and logical conclusion," is the immediate answer he gives to his own question. But the sense of logic seems faulty. The syllogism involved breaks down like this: Given, that our scribe copied a cosmopolitan melange of scholarly works; given, that a cosmopolitan gathering of scholars met in Basel; conclusion, the scribe worked in Basel. An analogistic case might be that of a hypothesist who, not knowing when or where Lincoln's "House-Divided" speech was delivered, might reason that since the speech was anti-secessionist in tone and that since a great gathering of anti-secessionist sentiment took place at the Republican convention of 1860 in Chicago, therefore the "House-Divided" speech was delivered in Chicago in 1860. But it was not: it was delivered at the Republican State Convention in Springfield, Illinois in 1858, defying, therefore, as so many facts do, "sensible and logical" conclusions that are merely vague hypothesizing.

Where else could such a triptych of works come together to be copied by a single scribe, the Vinland-Tartar book wants to know. The whole point of the rhetorical question quoted two paragraphs above—that the diversity of the three documents points to a cosmopolitan gathering, i.e. Basel—and a weak point it is at best, is completely nullified by the information, on p. 24 of the same book, that the triumvirate in Yale's library was not first brought together by the Basel scribe, but that he was merely copying a previous combination of the same three works (never found, of course). This comes in Mr. George D. Painter's portion of the book. Dr. Marston, meet Mr. Painter.

Copy or original, written left-handed or right-handed, by a monk or a lay scribe, what is there about the Vinland Map or either of its two supposed binding mates, to suggest that it was drawn at a church council? Nothing about it insists, even mildly, on an ecclesiastical atmosphere at its genesis. Does a mapmaker set up his easel to work in the midst of a parliamentary hubbub? The monk, if he was a monk, who copied the three works, if the same man did copy all three, could just as easily, and with a great deal more peace and quiet, have worked in his own cell, anywhere in Europe. Solitude is more congenial to the copyist than intellectual ferment.

By the beginning of the fifteenth century, civilization had well emerged from the gloom of the medieval centuries, never really wholly tenebrous. In the ecclesiastic communities the torches of learning had never been entirely spent, and after the 1200's these torches began to burn with a brightness that was a harbinger of the blazing noon of the Renaissance. The clerics carried their wisdom on all their travels over the face of the then-known earth, and when they met in world-wide councils, they exchanged with each other the nuggets they had extracted from the mines of their research.

If a map had actually appeared at the Church Council of Basel showing enormous new lands across the ocean, the reaction would have been as certain and as quick as that of a keg of gunpowder into which someone has tossed a match. It would have detonated rounds of excited discussion, addresses of laudation, singing of hosannahs, for if there was one thing that enlightened European man yearned for in that era it was more breathing space for the human race, an expansion in mind, spirit . . . and geography.

The backwash of the Crusades had expanded the horizons toward which the European sages looked. The great age of discovery—the age that reached its culmination in the voyages of Christopher Columbus—was just beyond the brink. Fear of the unknown kept the bold mariners of 1440 from venturing westward from the Azores, not a lack of curiosity. And a map of new lands introduced at the Church Council of Basel would have been more than an intellectual catalyst: it would have told the assembled clerics of new shores on which to plant the banners of Christianity, of possible heathen inhabitants to be brought into the fold of the Church. But no historian recorded any such stirring in the bosom of the Council, we have no letter written to announce the wonderful tidings by any delegate to a parishioner. Nor do the Vatican archives disclose any reference to a startling map of new lands, although reports were rendered to the Mother Church on all happenings at Basel.

Learned men from all over Europe came to this intellectual and ecclesiastical crossroads at Basel—the only place where, according to one of the two conflicting explanations offered in the Vinland-Tartar book, a medieval world history, an account of a journey deep into Asia, and a map embodying Scandinavian discoveries in the North Atlantic, could have come together to be bound as one. If such a map had been produced or exhibited at the Council, waves of excitement would have washed over Europe in the decades immediately following.

In 1484 Columbus approached John II, King of Portugal, and asked him for ships to sail westward in, and discover new land. Even in such an exploration-minded country as Portugal the project seemed visionary, but the King was interested, intrigued. He appointed a commission of illustrious scientists and churchmen who studied the plan and scoured Europe for the latest maps and geographical findings, but finally reported that the plan of the Genoese was not feasible. This did not deter the King from experimenting directly. He sent out two of his ablest sea captains to venture into the Atlantic and test Columbus' theory. They returned empty-handed, claiming that it was unthinkable to sail any further west into the uncharted ocean. Columbus went to Spain.

He stopped at a monastery where he was befriended by a Franciscan scholar, Antonio de Marchena. Although the Vatican kept all its ecclesiastical orders informed of such events, de Marchena had no news to offer Columbus of the display of a map of a "Vinland" across the western sea at the Council of Basel, forty-odd years before. De Marchena recommended to Columbus that he see Medina Celi, a wealthy shipowner of Cadiz, who in turn obtained an audience for him with King Ferdinand and Queen Isabella. The monarchs appointed a special learned commission, headed by the Queen's confessor, Hernando de Talavera, to consider the urgings of Columbus. For four years this commission inquired, studied maps, scrutinized reports of voyages. It is almost inevitable that they would have learned about a Vinland Map, if it had been produced at Basel, at least through the Spanish clericals in Rome. In 1490 the commission turned down Columbus' project on the grounds that it "rested on weak foundations."

We must remember, too, that Columbus and his brother Bartholomew were in the map business themselves. And, apart from the vast store of cartographic knowledge that came to Columbus through his profession, he acquired, on his marriage to Dona Felipa in 1479, a large collection of "writings and sea-charts" left by her father, Captain D. Bartholomew Perestrello, a seafarer of note thoroughly familiar with the "voyages and navigations that the Portuguese were making." But Columbus had no map of a great island to the west to help support the convictions he offered to the monarchs and their scholarly commissions.

Rejected by the courts of Portugal and Spain, Columbus dispatched Bartholomew, his brother, to the courts, first, of England, then of France, where the same story was repeated. The committees of experts appointed by Henry VII and Charles VIII, respectively, made the same sort of inquiries and arrived at the same pessimistic conclusion: there were no lands to be reached by sailing west.

The Portuguese, Spanish, British and French monarchs would have welcomed any opportunity to extend their territorial boundaries, to carry the Cross to a new corner of the world. But no ripples from Basel, no clarion call to adventure by a wonderful, strange map, dissipated in their minds the awesomeness of the ancient proverb: "Beyond all things, Ocean; beyond Ocean, nothing."

Either the fifteenth-century scholars at Basel were a good deal more sophisticated than some of their twentieth-century counterparts at New Haven, and found scant significance in a map illustrative of already-ancient Norse legend, or, as seems most likely to me, there was no Vinland Map at Basel.

Chapter 8

THE BIG BULL MARKET

If Yale's map is to prove that Leif Ericson landed on the grotesque piece of real estate labelled "Vinland" and that Columbus was merely a Chris-come-lately, the greater the show of certitude surrounding all aspects of the map's past the more awestruck and admiring the general public will be. It is difficult to doubt the pronouncements of experts when they seem, by their various specialist skills and labors, to be able to take an anonymous piece of cartographic doggerel from out of the blue and go so far as to assign it a date and place of origin. "Basel, about 1440" say the Yale experts, and if they know so much about it that they can even deduce with great show of certainty what town the monk did his copying in, why surely we can't doubt that the map is everything they say it is and proves everything they say it proves. At least, this is the attitude on the part of much of the public that the publicity and advertising surrounding the publication of the Vinland-Tartar book seem to take for granted.

The supposition that the map was copied in Basel rests on two premises. The first is the wholly gratuitous assumption, related in the preceding chapter, that the scribe must have been working at a church council. The second derives from a comparison of the paper used in the Tartar Relation and the Yale Speculum. You will remember the necessity for demonstrating, if the map is to be given a pre-Columbian date, that all three documents, map, Speculum and Tartar Relation, had originally been bound together after a common creation.

It is the contention first advanced by Laurence Witten, and supported by the editors of the Vinland-Tartar book, that the watermark on the paper in the Tartar Relation matched that of the watermark on the Speculum paper. The two watermarks are reproduced, the design being the head of a bull with what looks startlingly like a rooftop television antenna projecting from his head (it may only be a matter of time before someone asserts that this proves that television was invented in the fifteenth century). The watermark is identified as number 15056 in the reference work by Briquet on the subject, *Les Filigranes*. The burden of all this is that, according to the Vinland-Tartar book (p. 9), the identification of the paper is "primary evidence" in determining where and when the manuscripts were copied.

The expert witness called by the editors to clinch their case for Basel, Mr. Allan H. Stevenson, attempts to assign a date and place of manufacture of the paper on the basis of the watermarks. His letter is reproduced in full in the Vinland-Tartar book, with no further comment on the part of the editors, who seem to feel that the letter establishes their case. Actually, with refreshing candor, Mr. Stevenson, at the end of a highly technical discussion, demonstrates the impossibility of assigning a specific date and place of manufacture of the paper on the basis of the watermarks. Discussing the locales at which the Spectacled Bull (the particular form of bullshead design involved here) may have been made, he arrives at this conclusion: "Of the three sources around 1440, Piedmont, Fribourg, Basel, the chances seem but slightly to favor Basel."

Hardly a ringing endorsement of the Basel theory, but it might be unfair to expect more positive expert testimony in any case because, according to the Quebec, Canada, handwriting and document expert, Raymond Dubé:

> "There were many imitations as well as many unintended coincidences and the numerous variants render difficult any attempt to determine the origin and epoch of a paper from the watermarks alone. In addition, the period of use of one and the same watermark varied." (personal communication)

Even if the mill supplying the paper for the Speculum and Tartar Relation could be fixed at Basel with far greater certainty than is the case, it would not establish that the manuscripts were actually copied there, since any one paper mill might supply a substantial geographical area.

It must also be borne in mind that the Vinland Map itself is parchment, not paper, and that any connection that can be proven between the other two works on the basis of paper has no bearing on the claims to legitimacy of the map. There are intermittent parchment leaves in both the Yale Speculum and the Tartar Relation and the editors endeavor to guess at some similarity between the map parchment and one of the leaves of manuscript parchment. However, they object to submitting their documents to any chemical tests, objecting that none is accurate enough to be useful, and that all involve destruction of a fragment of the parchment.

More and more, the habitation of our "possibly left-handed" monk, so confidently awarded to Basel, appears to be erected upon a scaffolding of mere guesswork.

Tilting their leaning tower of guesswork another degree or two, the Vinland-Tartar editors claim that the handwriting in their Speculum manuscript proves it to be by the same copyist who drew the map and copied the Tartar Relation.

The handwriting referred to is not handwriting in the sense that the term is used today, when every individual develops his own peculiarities of style. Printing had not yet been invented when our anonymous copyist supposedly wrote, and the dissemination of literature was dependent on scribes laboriously copying out manuscripts by hand. The copyist of that period was in effect a human Xerox machine. His hand conformed to a standard style that it might be intelligible to the reader, free of personal idiosyncrasy. He used printing rather than script, printing being both more legible and much easier to duplicate without noticeable variation. Even today, it is simpler to imitate a person's printing accurately than his script.

On page 6 of the Vinland-Tartar book, the handwriting of the Yale Speculum and the Tartar Relation is identified with the almost overwhelming style classification of "Oberrheinische Bastarda," and a date is assigned as "most appropriate" for it: the 1440's. In the case of the Speculum, "a few additional notes have been added in a cursive humanistic script of about 1500." These notes are brushed off with the declaration that "These later notations are so trivial as to be without significance." Any clue pointing to a post-Columbian date receives very short shrift in the Yale University Press volume. The assumption is made, quite gratuitously, that writing in an admitted 1500 manner must have been added later. The possibility that the bulk of the text was copied much later than the 1440's is not discussed.

If one will look in the Vinland-Tartar book at the photographs of the pages of the Yale Speculum and the Tartar Relation, he will see at once that the type of writing there reproduced is not by any means confined to the 1440's or to any specific subsequent period. This type of writing is also called engrossing, and is commonly seen in the preparation of diplomas, testimonials, citations and official greetings. A skilled engrosser would have no difficulty in making a letter-perfect duplicate of a specimen of an earlier period, the style of the Speculum being no exception.

Dr. Marston deduces from the writing in the manuscripts that the anonymous scribe apparently wrote out the Tartar Relation very hurriedly, as if the copyist only had brief access to his model, while the Speculum shows no such signs of haste, being in the copyist's best neatness-counts manner. It seems strange that our mysterious monk should be in such a rush to complete the 32-page Tartar Relation, yet be dawdling along in a leisurely way in the third fat volume of a multiple-volume encyclopedia totalling 1,450,000 words.

Here again, though, even granting the map's proponents the benefit of the doubt, their argument does not prove the genuineness or date of the map, which is the crux of the matter if we are to revise the facts of the discovery of America on its basis. The resemblance between the writing in the Tartar Relation and the Yale Speculum means nothing unless an identity be proved between their script and that of the inscriptions on the Vinland Map.

You may wonder just what even this would prove. If we had a painting showing a scribe copying the Vinland Map with his left hand while copying the Tartar Relation with his right hand, would this documentation of ambidextrous virtuosity prove that Columbus didn't discover America?

The captioning of the map, as a matter of fact, is extremely tiny, making an intelligent identification of it with the large, sprawling "upper Rhineland Bastard" script of the manuscript a very touchy undertaking. The identification is, of course, confidently asserted in the Vinland-Tartar book, but the London *Sunday Times* article previously cited reports on a meeting in London of the Society of Antiquaries on February 24, 1966, under the chairmanship of the noted paleographer, Professor Francis Wormald of London University:

> "The record of the meeting has not been published, but the general feeling of the discussion was that, while the script on the Map and the Relation could be contemporary in style, there were reservations about their being by the same hand. Differences in the scaling and spacing of the letters were pointed out. The consensus was that further evidence—such as chemical analysis of inks, etc.—would be required before the authors' premise could be accepted."

A final thought on the matter of the handwriting: Dr. Marston, in a poignant passage admitting the difficulty of dating a manuscript through the style of writing (pp. 6–7), admits that a copyist might well live a very long time and move from place to place, not changing his writing the whole time, so that even if two specimens can be assumed to be by the same scribe, this is no guarantee that they were written within hundreds of miles of the same place or scores of years of the same time.

As to the fifteenth-century binding which encloses the Yale Speculum, and which the editors of the Vinland-Tartar book contend once joined all three works, the editors offer nothing more edifying than the statement that the binding is unique in its mingling of German and Italian techniques, thus making comparison with bindings of known origin impossible. No guess is offered as to where it was made, but the inevitable pre-Columbian date is assigned.

What a shame that such a blockbuster of genuine erudition and technical detail is turned loose against a little parchment map, trying to push it into a firm niche in history . . . only to fail. The Vinland Map is a baby left on our doorstep without a note, unless we count the sensation-mongering little *billet-doux* from Yale's publicity department that tried to steal Columbus' thunder.

Chapter 9

THE TARTAR SAUCE
ON THE VINLAND HASH

Samuel Eliot Morison, in his New York *Times* review of the Vinland-Tartar book, well observed that the presentation of the Vinland Map "has been used as a stick to beat down the reputation of Columbus."

The whole emphasis of the Yale University Press, in its exploitation of map and book, has been on the Vikings and Columbus, on America or "Vinland." In view of this, it seems very strange that, out of a total of 262 pages of text in *The Vinland Map and the Tartar Relation,* fully 88 are devoted to Russia and the land of the Tartars, as well as copious references elsewhere in the book. These 88 pages contain the full text of the Tartar Relation in Latin, translation with an awesome battery of footnotes, and an article of explication. In addition to all this, on unnumbered pages are photographic reproductions of the complete Tartar manuscript.

What have central Asia and the exploits of the Mongols to do with the discovery of America? No more than with flights to Mars. But since the Vinland Map requires some thematic relationship with at least one of the two manuscripts with which it was allegedly copied and bound, for Yale's theory of its origin to be acceptable, a bridge of surmise had to be erected between Vinland and the Gobi Desert.

The Vinland-Tartar editors hold that the map was intended to illustrate the Speculum Historiale, but they have to admit a complete lack of specific reference in the map to the encyclopedic history of Father Vincent of Beauvais.

The Speculum, remember, in its complete form consists of 32 books relating the story of the world from Creation to the date of publication, 1255. It was compiled by one of the most learned men of his age, and embodies, in its 1,450,000 words of text, an enormous array of sources. Leif Ericson is supposed to have reached our shores in 1000 A.D., following the supposed accidental landfall of Bjarni Herjolfsson. A number of other journeys are averred to have followed Leif's to North America, and it is claimed also that an actual, though ephemeral, settlement was begun. Yet not one word of any of this exploration, discovery, settlement, and abandonment of a Norse colony on a great land across the Atlantic appears in the Speculum of Friar Vincent!

If the Vinland Map scribe was also, as it is asserted, the copyist of Yale's text of the Speculum, it is a fair assumption that he had some awareness of what he was copying. It is difficult to write without knowing how to read what you are writing, a feat accomplished only, so far as I know, by the animals in the comicstrip *Pogo*. A number of descriptive or historical allusions appear among the captions on the map, including the references to Leif, Bjarni, and Bishop Eirik. But not a word that specifically connects the encyclopedia with the map alleged to illustrate it; and the feature making this map unique among all maps produced at the time, its depiction of huge new land across the western sea, lies completely outside the vast scope of the Speculum. If North America was known to Europeans in the Middle Ages, Father Vincent, who, more than anybody else, should have had that knowledge, was blissfully unaware of it.

Father Vincent's lack of acquaintance with Vinland and the general irrelevance of his text to the material on the map left those attempting to verify the map with the task of establishing its consanguinity with the Tartar Relation. Not that the latter offered tales of Vinland and the Vikings, of course, but a case could be put by the Yale editors for a correlation between the manuscript and the Asiatic portions of the map on a chronological basis.

This offered another advantage, besides bolstering the arguments for the map's 1440ish date. It gave the Yale Univer-

sity Press the opportunity to couple publication of the Vinland
Map with that of the Tartar Relation, which otherwise would
have come to the attention of only a tiny number of specialists.
Now the entire arsenal of scholarly ammunition—text, translation, manuscript reproduction, footnotes, cross-references,
exegesis—could be marshaled to bowl over the reader—and to
pad out the book. Anyone wishing to get the full story of the
Vinland Map and how it is supposed to prove the discovery of
America five centuries before Columbus, must also take with it
an 88-page section devoted to a second-hand account of a thir-
teenth-century mission to the Mongols.

The erudition displayed in Yale's presentation of the Tartar Relation in the book is truly splendid. But for the reader
who is not a specialist in medieval history—and a rather esoteric
subdivision of medieval history at that—the inclusion of all this
in a book advertised as disproving Columbus' discovery of
America fills the air with the faint aroma of the crimson
herring. The material evinced to demonstrate the supposed
physical and textual association between the Tartar manuscript
and the Vinland Map is fulsomely brought out in other sections
of the Vinland-Tartar book.

The Tartar Relation is not even a document of primary
importance in medieval history, being a second-hand rendering
of a description of Asia that has come down to us first-hand. In
the year 1245, Pope Innocent IV sent three Franciscan monks,
Friar John de Plano Carpini, Benedict the Pole, and Ceslaus of
Bohemia, on a mission to central Asia with the ultimate goal of
converting the great Mongol Khan to the Christian faith. In
this respect the mission failed, but the friars, on their return
through Europe, stopped at various places giving lectures on
what they had seen. Eventually, Carpini himself incorporated
the narrative of the journey and all that he had learned about
the Tartar peoples and other peoples of Asia into a book, *Historia Mongalorum*. Friar Benedict, too, committed his version
of the odyssey to writing.

The Tartar Relation presented by the Yale Press, however,
is neither of these. It is a transcription, by a Franciscan friar,
one C. de Bridia, of one of the lectures given by Friar Benedict

on the return through Europe. Nothing is known about De Bridia, not even his first name, although the Vinland-Tartar book postulates, from his handling of his material, that he had a "second-rate mind."

Why did anyone find it necessary to couple this Tartar Relation in a binding with the Speculum Historiale? When Father Carpini returned from central Asia he was sent by the Pope to the royal court of King Louis IX of France, and there Carpini's account of his journey and of the Asiatic peoples came into the hands of Father Vincent of Beauvais, engaged at the time in writing his great Speculum. Friar Vincent incorporated, in abridged form, Carpini's account in Book 32, the last book, of his encyclopedia. So, with the inclusion in the Speculum of material deriving at first hand from the head of the very mission described, it makes very little sense that an inept, second-hand account, omitting the narrative sections of the journey, should be thought worth copying by hand and binding with the Speculum.

There are several other curious points about the juxtaposition of the two manuscripts, a juxtaposition so vital for establishing the pre-Columbian date of Yale's parchment map. One is that no other extant copy of the Speculum Historiale includes this addendum of the Tartar Relation. It is obviously not sanctioned by the Speculum's author, it lacks precedent as well as good sense.

Another is that, if the Tartar Relation were to be bound, as a sort of appendix, to a volume of the Speculum, it would certainly be with the volume containing Book 32, the book which includes the story of the Carpini mission. But Yale's sole volume of the Speculum ends with Book 24. This whole problem of the utter lack of chronological relevance of the Tartar Relation and the Vinland Map to the material of the Speculum volume with which they are alleged to have been bound, will be reviewed in the next chapter. But for now, let me just raise one more unanswered question: considering the unimportance of the Tartar Relation compared to the entire Speculum Historiale, why would the sketcher of a map intended to illustrate the Speculum take his captions from the Tartar Relation?

As for the reliability of the Tartar Relation as a historical or geographical document, perhaps the most charitable way of putting it is to say that it is in a class with the Vinland Map! Either some very peculiar events were transpiring in central Asia in the thirteenth century, or the Tartar Relation stands as a monument to the gullibility of certain Europeans.

Here are a few of the episodes related in the Tartar Relation:

A mountain in the Caspians is so charged with magnetic power that all iron objects, even including the horseshoes on the horses, fly towards it violently;

In a Land of Dogs, where the females are human but the males are all, literally, dogs, the Tartars lose a battle in what may be the sire of all shaggy dog stories: the shaggy-coated dogs, before the battle, wet themselves and roll in sand, and—the weather being freezing—become completely coated with a mixture of ice and sand that renders them impregnable to the Tartar arrows;

A people called the Parossits eat nothing but steam, ingested through a "minute orifice" in place of the usual mouth; when they stew meat, they just inhale the steam and throw the meat to their dogs;

A people called the Ucorcolon or Nochoyterim have feet like oxen and faces like dogs; when they talk, every third word is barked;

The Unipeds, a race of men with one hand and one foot, are the best shots with the bow and arrow of any nation, and can outrun a horse or any other animal! (You may be pleased to learn that we will encounter the Unipeds again, one of them, anyhow, who was an early immigrant to Vinland.)

If only Father Carpini had brought along his camera! In fairness to the good friars, however, it should be pointed out that they do not claim to have observed all these wonders themselves . . . they had them on the good authority of their Asiatic hosts.

Perhaps the most pertinent comment on the value of all this comes from the Vinland-Tartar book itself (p. 51), where Mr. George D. Painter candidly offers that "our chief gratitude to Friar Benedict and his editor C. de Bridia is due, perhaps, to their unwitting collaboration, nearly two centuries later, in the compilation of the Vinland Map."

Parossits, Ucorcolons and Unipeds aside, do the captions on the Vinland Map necessitate the assumption that it had a common copyist with the Tartar Relation?

Mr. R. A. Skelton, in his portion of the Yale Press book, seems to be rather nonplussed by the mapmaker's use of captions in the Asian part of his work. Failing to link the placement of the captions with either a logical geographical plan or with the chronology of Father Carpini's expedition, Mr. Skelton is forced to concede that the drawer of the map simply threw in his captions wherever he had enough space.

Nevertheless, the Yale editors argue the common origin of the map and the particular manuscript copy of the Relation. Besides being a necessary brick in the structure of tortuous reasoning whereby they seek to prove the Viking discovery of America, the editors claim that the Tartar Relation can give us an idea of the "intentions, resources, and psychology of the Vinland Map's compiler."

If it was one of our anonymous penman's intentions to illustrate, with his map, the Tartar Relation, then either he made very inadequate use of his resources or something was radically wrong with his psychology. The Vinland-Tartar book lists and translates 67 captions from the Vinland Map. I count 30 captions for parts of the world coming generally within the area covered by the Carpini expedition. If the Vinland Map was sketched to illustrate the Tartar Relation, it is reasonable to expect a strong percentage of coincidence between these captions and the equivalent material in the Relation.

Of the 30 critical captions, 24 are simply place names, with no descriptive or historical notes. Of these, just eight would seem to agree with the terminology used in the Tartar Relation; the other sixteen refer, in whole or in part, to places not mentioned in the Tartar Relation, except for two which have counterparts in the Relation but where a discrepancy exists in spelling or geographical placement between map and Tartar Relation.

The other six captions are actually brief notes of geographical or historical information. Although some elements in them agree with corresponding passages in the Tartar Relation, each of them, wholly or partly, brings in material either not included in the Tartar Relation or in contradiction with it. An example is the caption (No. 30) referring to the land of the mythical Prester John, a Christian king who reigned tantalizingly in the imaginations of medieval Europeans. Some legends put him in Asia, others in Africa; although none could locate his kingdom, many Christians looked to him as an ally in the Crusades against the followers of Islam. The Tartar Relation locates Prester John in Asia; the Vinland Map puts him in Africa.

(For the benefit of anyone wishing to make these comparisons for himself, I considered the following captions relevant to the geographical area covered by the Tartar Relation, using the caption numbers in the Vinland-Tartar book: all those in the Asian section of the map except Jerusalem and Mecca, which the cartographer would obviously know about in any case; 30, in Africa, the Prester John caption; and 8, 9, and 12 in eastern Europe, eliminating caption 11, Russia, since the name also appears in 12. Nos. 8, 40, 42, 43, 44, 45, 47, and 48 are the captions involving no discrepancy with the Relation text, although the agreement does not, of course, mean that the drawer of the map could not have learned these names from other sources, including Carpini's own narrative of his expedition.)

Hardly a clinching case for the intimate association of the Vinland Map with the Tartar Relation. Nor can even those who discern a closer textual parallel between the two than I do, see in this any guarantee of the joint copying of the two documents: a mapmaker, working at a much later period, might have drawn some of his notions from an already aged copy of the de Bridia text.

We will draw our final quotation for this chapter from Mr. Painter in the Vinland-Tartar book. Lamenting that the anonymous mapmaker used only the first half of the de Bridia text in preparing his chart, Mr. Painter points out that "the compiler shows a strikingly unscientific disregard for the Tartar Relation as an objective source of information" (p. 244).

Naturally, he was being scientific when he drew Vinland.

Chapter 10

VINLAND MAPS AND VINLAND MAPS

The whole chain of reasoning that leads Yale's team of experts to the conclusion that their map dates from about 1440 and proves the discovery of Western Hemisphere mainland prior to the journeys of Columbus, as we have seen, depends upon one link being firmly in place: the presence, in the same binding and at their inception, of the Vinland Map, Tartar Relation, and Yale Speculum.

We have examined the several arguments put forth—the wormholes, handwriting, paper, textual references in the map, and others—finding, in my opinion, that none of them lends adequate support to Yale's theory. Their value, as proof of the pre-Columbian date and the genuineness of the map, ranges from absolutely zero to dubious. At best, such evidence as that of the handwriting and the paper does not disprove Yale's thesis. At worst, evidence such as that of the anachronistic cartography, with its slick Greenland appended to a medieval Europe, points in the very opposite direction, and evidence such as that of the wormholes verges on low comedy.

But all of these arguments, received in the most charitable manner, go down the drain of empty conjecture if Yale cannot somehow get that map and that encyclopedia together in one set of covers. The question of the relevance of the map and the Tartar Relation to Yale's sole Speculum volume has been touched upon in the last chapter; we will now look at it from another point of view.

First, a quick review of the physical facts about Yale's

Speculum volume. The original encyclopedic work, you will re-member, was numbered at 32 books; there is no standard num-ber of volumes into which it is divided. The single volume of the Yale Speculum contains books 21 through 24, and it is their belief, arrived at by estimating the number of sheets missing and the amount of text they would carry, that the volume originally included books 20 through 24. On the last page is written "here ends the third part of the Speculum Historiale." The other volumes of this particular copying have yet to come to light (there is of course no guarantee that the copyist ever finished his job, but it is a fair assumption).

The only textual indication that the Vinland Map is re-lated to *any* edition of the Speculum is the notation, on the back of the map, "Delineation of the first part, the second part (and) the third part of the Speculum." There is absolutely no indication in the text of the Tartar Relation that it was ever in-tended to accompany the Speculum or the Vinland Map.

Considering the map, there are only two reasonable hy-potheses as to where it should have been placed in a multi-volume edition of the Speculum. The inscription on the back of the map would seem to point most sensibly to placement at the very beginning of the text, since it offers itself as an illustration of the first three parts. Can this be correct? If it is, and if Yale's contention about the map being of 1440 vintage is to be up-held, then we must accept an extraordinary achievement on the part of our three most persevering bookworms: they chewed their way through the Vinland Map, the first two thick volumes of the Speculum, containing 19 books as well as the leather bindings, the front cover of the third volume (leaving no hole behind them!), the missing book 20 and part way into the re-mainder! Surely a journey to put Phileas Fogg's around-the-world-in-eighty-days trip into the shade. And, even more re-markable, the ravenous little beasts, after gourmandizing their way through all those millennia of the world's history, came out in practically the same formation as when they started, and within a few leaves of each other.

This is too much for Yale's experts, as well as the worms, to swallow. So we are left with the alternative hypothesis: the Vinland Map was placed by the bookbinder in the particular volume containing the accounts of the events supposedly referred to in the map's captions. But Friar Vincent's text contains not a word about Vinland . . . and if only the captions bearing a rather fuzzy relevance to Father Carpini's mission are considered, then the map belongs with the last (missing) volume, which holds the events of part of the thirteenth century. This hypothesis would be consistent with the map being bound into the same volume as the Tartar Relation.

But the map, by its own notation, illustrates parts one, two and three only . . . and volume three is the one in Yale's library, carrying the story of the world only up to the year 801 A.D. (The Carpini mission was in 1245–47).

As Jimmy Durante might say, "What a dilemma!"

The Vinland Map and the Tartar Relation do not go with the Yale Speculum volume. The worms, summoned so confidently by Mr. Witten and Yale's board of inquiry, have committed perjury!

But wait a minute . . . there is a way out of this, a way in which it can be argued that the map, after all, did accompany the two manuscripts in the same binding. It involves a wholly arbitrary and excruciatingly involved set of assumptions on the part of the map's proponents. It is up to you to decide whether this plaintive excursion into the wild blue yonder of supposition can properly be used to support the historic pronouncements so blatantly trumpeted on Columbus Day, 1965.

The chain of imagined events that is offered to show how the Vinland Map could have been bound into the wrong volume of the Speculum is glossed over by Mr. Painter on pages 26–27 of the Vinland-Tartar book. The passage is really a dazzler: so elliptical in style that anyone fully comprehending at his first reading exactly what the Yale team is hypothesizing deserves a prize. Throughout the entire Yale argument, there is the constant emphasis on the inseparability of the Vinland Map, the Yale Speculum, and the Tartar Relation. They are the unseverable *Three Musketeers,* the *Three Men in a Boat, The Three Sisters,* the *Three Soldiers.* Yet Mr. Painter himself upsets the whole apple cart of this trilogy when he says that the

Vinland Map makes no sense in the volume in which it is ensconced at Yale because there is no believable relation between the two.

Yale's hypothesis begins by forcing upon the reader the assumption that the Vinland Map, so proudly displayed in the Yale Beinecke Library as the "earliest known and indisputable cartographic representation" of America, is not the original Vinland Map at all, but a copy of an earlier one which was also bound together with a Speculum Historiale and a Tartar Relation. Further, that this in turn was a copy of a *still* earlier Vinland Map, also bound with the same two works. Needless to say, none of these older books and maps have ever been found. They exist only as fantasies conjured from the air as necessary components of Yale's argument.

We are then asked by Mr. Painter to assume that the oldest of these Map-Speculum-Tartar combinations was bound in three volumes, the middle combination in four volumes, and the last, the one which in part rests in Yale's Library, was bound in five volumes. We are even asked to assume that the Yale Speculum volume was the fourth of the five volumes, despite its inscription ("here ends the third part . . ."). Why? Because the scribe, the monk at Basel, erroneously copied the inscription from the hypothetical four-volume set!

Yet more assumptions: We must assume the bookbinder who covered the Yale Speculum misconstrued the inscription, thought *this* must be the "third part of the Speculum" that the map was supposed to delineate, and so inserted the map into the wrong volume.

But why did the map carry its notation about illustrating the first, second and third parts? According to the Yale hypothesis, remember, the Yale Speculum belonged to a five-volume edition, and the Vinland Map would only make sense either at the very beginning, or in the last volume, as we saw. All that's necessary for us to reconcile the map's notation with the Yale theory is that we make three more assumptions. First, that the notation was originally put on the prototype Vinland Map, the one supposed to accompany the imagined three-volume Speculum. Second, that the notation was erroneously copied when the hypothetical second Vinland Map was drawn, the one alleged to have been bound with a four-volume Speculum. Finally, we must assume that, by a very strange coincidence, the exact same error was made by the monk at Basel when he made *his* copy of the map.

A veritable comedy of errors, all purely hypothetical, and an inundation of Speculums, all now lost, leaving not a rack behind. But, if you are willing to go along with so many groundless assumptions, you can at last have—if you want it— your Yale Speculum volume, with the world's history from 411 to 801 A.D., sheltering between its covers the silly map, with its prattle about Leif and Bjarni, circa 1000 A.D., and, we are told, also about the Carpini/Tartar story from the mid-thirteenth century. But after Yale's team has gone to such lengths to get its map and Speculum volume together—conjuring up, out of such stuff as dreams are made on, its plethora of scribes and binders strewing encyclopedias with misinserted maps all over the medieval landscape—it seems almost ungrateful to have to ask them: how come the Tartar Relation also wound up in that same wrong volume? Their theory doesn't even attempt to answer that.

We must take the misplacement of the Tartar Relation as a matter of faith, since Yale offers no explanation for it. And if we are to accept the Vinland Map as a plausible pre-Columbian document, even though it is at such drastic variance with any other known map of its period, we have to accept the existence of two other Vinland Maps which have never been found. Examine the ladder of supposition raised by Yale to climb to its goal of endorsing the Viking discovery of America, examine each rung: the imagined three-volume set, the imagined four-volume set, the two imagined Vinland Maps, the imagined and unexplained quirk of the Tartar Relation for winding up in the wrong binding, the imagined errors of the scribes and binder. Contrast this structure of "ifs" and "supposes" and "let's assumes" with the supreme cockiness of the press release of Columbus Day, guaranteeing to all Americans the veracity of the legendary voyages to America by the Norsemen, guaranteeing them through the "eight years of painstaking research by British and American experts to establish the authenticity of the earliest and only pre-Columbian map now in existence showing any part of the Western Hemisphere."

Of course, there is a simpler explanation: Columbus discovered America.

Besides being such a weak and contrived argument in itself, the Yale explanation for the map being bound with the wrong volume of the Speculum completely yanks the carpet out from under another of their confident assertions: the vivid word-picture in the Vinland-Tartar book of the busy monk copying his works in the midst of the great intellectual ferment of the Church Council at Basel. Where else, Yale wanted to know, could three such disparate items come together for a common copying, a medieval encyclopedic history, a world map with undoubted Scandinavian sources, and a report of a journey to Karakorum in Mongolia. And the answer came back: Basel.

But if the three works had been collected together at least twice before, why should one assume that the scribe of Yale's manuscript must have been working in an international cosmopolitan atmosphere in Basel? The Yale University Press book does not even offer a guess as to where the hypothetical three-volume combination of Speculum and Vinland Map was copied.

The poignancy of having to base the claim for the authenticity of the Vinland Map on the purely hypothetical existence of two earlier Vinland Maps bound into two earlier encyclopedias, is nowhere better exemplified than in the words of Mr. Painter in the Vinland-Tartar book (p. 27): "The remote but exciting possibility remains that the present publication may lead to the discovery of a hitherto unnoticed three-volume Speculum Historiale manuscript complete with the original Vinland Map and an earlier Tartar Relation. Perhaps it is too much to hope that such a manuscript might also include as an additional appendix the unknown source for the Vinland area and captions of the Map. But it would at least be likely to provide a more correct version of the Vinland Map and a less corrupt text of the Tartar Relation."

If it ever does show up, there's no doubt when it will be publicly announced.

Columbus Day.

Chapter 11

"HISTORY" IS MADE AT YALE

How valuable can the Vinland Map be as a historic document? Taking the most charitable attitude toward its authenticity, should history books be revised because of it, should Columbus be demoted and Leif and Bjarni raised to national herohood?

I would like to summarize, in tabular form, a thorough analysis I have read of the obstacles to be considered by anyone wishing to rewrite history on the authority of the Vinland Map:

1) The map has no date.

2) The map does not carry the name of its originator or its copyist.

3) There is no indication where it was made.

4) It is eclectic in style: no known map can be singled out as its source, no geographical tradition adduced as its inspiration.

5) Material on the map apparently comes from texts which haven't survived to the present.

6) Both the cartography and the captions of the map point to ideas and incidents of a much earlier date than that at which the map was allegedly drawn; the mapmaker had to use material that was itself second-hand at best, and sometimes even further from the source.

7) Not only are the sources for the map untraced in part, but the personality of the map's author intervenes between them and the modern researcher: the editorial caprices, as it

72

were, of the mapmaker in choosing and modifying his material cannot be appreciated.

This judiciously reasoned analysis does not come from one of the map's detractors, from a hostile review of the Vinland-Tartar book, or from the director of the Italian Historical Society of America. It comes from the Vinland-Tartar book itself, specifically from the section of the book contributed by Mr. R. A. Skelton, Superintendent of the Map Room in the British Museum. Mr. Skelton concurs with the other gentlemen selected by the Yale University Press to prepare the book in the general view that the Vinland Map is, in its present form, a genuine pre-Columbian document, and that it is evidence for the supposition that Viking voyages to America preceded those of Christopher Columbus. Nevertheless, the candor with which Mr. Skelton sets forth the difficulties confronting even the map's proponents when attempting to make of it a historical document, contrasts refreshingly with the barrage of unmitigated drivel that accompanied the book's publication on Columbus Day, 1965.

"In effect, the map proved that the hardy Norsemen had explored the northern American coastlands by that time [1440]," said the press release that wormed its way onto so many front pages, in a recital of tub-thumping far more appropriate to a detergent commercial.

I believe that, within a short time, the Vinland Map will have, in scholarly precincts, the same status as a historical document as another manuscript relating to Columbus: the parchment, as its promoter claimed, on which Columbus himself had written the story of his first voyage. By a happy coincidence, it turned up in 1892, the 400th anniversary of the discovery of the New World. The promoter had picked it up, he said, from a fisherman off the coast of Wales, and it was the very parchment that Columbus had thrown into the sea, in a sealed cask, when the *Nina,* carrying him back to Spain, was in danger of foundering in a severe storm. The parchment, so that it might be better understood, according to this promoter, had been written in English!

Nowhere in its 291-page volume can the Yale University

Press committee of experts offer an unassailable, cogent reason for accepting their map as a brick in the house of history. The arguments brought forth to "prove" the map—to prove it a genuine document, to prove it pre-Columbian in date, and to prove it an authentic record of historical events—not only fail to stand up to rigorous examination but they even contend among themselves. The map, according to the very theory so ingeniously worked out by the Yale team to account for its inclusion in the wrong volume of the Speculum text, is:

a copy by an unknown scribe of:

another copy not known to exist by another unknown scribe of:

still another map not known to exist by still another unknown scribe working in an unknown place at an unknown time and getting his information from unknown sources.

As a historical document, the map offered by Yale could hardly be less trustworthy if it plainly showed Disneyland.

As late as 1960, three years after the unveiling of the Vinland Map, Mr. Skelton of Yale's team had this to say, in a chapter he contributed to *The Journal of Christopher Columbus,* published by Clarkson N. Potter, Inc., New York:

> "The earliest world maps to depict the discoveries in the West, including those of Columbus' first voyage, dated from the period immediately after his return from the third voyage; these are the Spanish map of La Cosa (1500), the Portuguese 'Cantino' map (1502), and the Italian 'Canerio' map drawn from a Portuguese prototype similar to Cantino."

In the Vinland-Tartar book, Mr. Skelton is forced to conclude that the body of water at the head of the more northerly inlet of "Vinland" is a "cartographic convention" (p. 216). Antillia and Satanaxes are cartographic conventions. Italy, on this 1440 map, has had its foot amputated, although its boot-like shape is clearly depicted on the Ptolemy map of the world of 150 A.D., and with splendid accuracy on a 1311 map of Petrus Vesconte. But the fine smooth hand of the Vinland Map sketcher can produce a Greenland that shrieks twentieth century!

Mr. Painter in the Vinland-Tartar book (pp. 251–252):

> "The outline of Greenland, in view of its extraordinary accuracy, has presumably suffered little alteration. But the portrayal of Vinland, it may well seem, has the air of being the end product of a long process of exaggeration . . . The archetype itself was doubtless a mere inference from the saga tradition, a schematic representation retaining no real link with geographical experience."

How can a copyist's doodle even be called a map if it bears "no real link with geographical experience?" The very word "map" must be redefined to fit the Vinland Fantasy. And the word "history" must be redefined if it is to embrace such ambivalent documents as a map whose Greenland, drawn from hypothetical Norse records, is accepted *because* it is so accurate, and whose Vinland, inches away, is accepted *despite* having no connection with the "geographical experience" of the same hypothetical records.

A scrap of parchment bears what is apparently a mediocre medieval world map that has suffered a suspicious sea change somewhere between the never-never land of its birth and the Beinecke Library in New Haven. But not content with exhibiting it as the mere unverified cartographic curio it is, those responsible for the custody of the map at Yale have succumbed to the temptation of slitting open their ungainly goose of a map to extract the golden egg of publicity and sensationalism.

Part II

THE NORSE SAGAS

Chapter 12

SOURCE FOR THE GOOSE

On the eve of Columbus Day, 1965, to herald the announcement of the Vinland Map, Yale's News Bureau fired its salvo of positive-sounding claims, proofs and deductions, most of which turned out to be much bolder in their assertiveness than the blanks of academic guesswork fired in the book itself. The map, the press release informed the world, "was made from source materials which date back at least to the 13th century." What are these source materials? Earlier maps? Yale, as we have seen, postulates two, produces none; and even if they could produce their hypothetical Vinland Map prototypes, these would not be first-hand cartographic documentations. The source for the Vinland Map must ultimately lie in the records, graphic or verbal, made by the Norse seafarers themselves, and the only ones that the map's proponents can point to, rather than merely assume to have existed, are the Norse sagas.

Of course the Vinland Map itself now becomes source material for those anxious to confirm their theories of pre-Columbian discovery of our shores. We will review, in these next chapters, the support given the Vinland Map by the sagas, the support given the sagas by the Vinland Map, and the support given the claim, by both map and sagas, that as historical fact credit for the discovery of the New World goes to Leif Ericson and company.

Admitting the Vinland Map into a discussion of source materials for the writing of history is like admitting a beggar to a society ball. But for now we will accept it as one of the three documents on which the Viking discovery of America is predicated, the other two being the *Saga of Eirik the Red* and the *Greenlanders' Saga*. Do these sources support and confirm each other?

The Vinland Map has two captions relating to this subject. As translated in the Vinland-Tartar book, they are:

> "Island of Vinland, discovered by Bjarni and Leif in company."
>
> "By God's will, after a long voyage from the island of Greenland to the south toward the most distant remaining parts of the western ocean sea, sailing southward amidst the ice, the companions Bjarni and Leif Eiriksson discovered a new land, extremely fertile and even having vines, the which island they named Vinland. Eric, legate of the Apostolic See and bishop of Greenland and the neighboring regions, arrived in this truly vast and very rich land, in the name of Almighty God, in the last year of our most blessed father Paschal, remained a long time in both summer and winter, and later returned northeastward toward Greenland and then proceeded in most humble obedience to the will of his superiors."

The Vinland-Tartar book offers its other ancient references to the Bishop, principally from the Icelandic Annals, but admits the lack of confirmation for the scant mentions of him, including a reference to his supposed death in Vinland, which would seem to conflict with the material about Eric on the map.

Professor Gustav Storm of Copenhagen, a noted authority on the sagas, has said that in the Icelandic Annals

> ". . . the bishop does not go to Vineland, he merely sets out (from Greenland) in search of the country. The most natural explanation of these words is, that he did not find it; either he turned back home without

having attained his object, or the ship was lost . . .
To any connection therefore with Vineland, the voy-
age of Bishop Eirik did not lead." (*Studies on the
Vineland Voyages,* Copenhagen, 1888)

(I must pause here to ask the reader's indulgence in my
practice of retaining, in my quotations from other books, their
authors' spellings of the Norse names. There is no definitive
rendering of these names for contemporary writing in English,
hence the good Bishop may be Eirik here and Eric there, the
land he may or may not have visited is Vinland in one place,
Vineland in another.)

As we will see, one saga makes Bjarni Herjolfsson the
accidental discoverer of Vinland, fifteen years before Leif's arrival, the other saga omits him from the sweepstakes altogether.
How does the map solve this riddle? By putting Bjarni and Leif
together! Fair? maybe, but history? no. We now have the amus-
ing spectacle of a map getting its confirmation from two stories,
at the same time that the two stories are being verified by the
map, and all three of them in complete conflict.

Don't think for a minute that this greatly abashes the
Vinland-Tartar book, which offers this splendid bit of side-
stepping: "The legend in the Vinland Map, if it faithfully re-
produces a genuine record, accordingly authenticates Bjarni's
association with the discovery of Vinland and adds the significant information that he sailed with Leif."

There is something almost wistful in the use of words such
as "authenticates" and "significant information" to describe a
caption that is at utter variance with what it is supposed to
verify.

As verification for the Norse discovery of America, as inferred from the sagas, the Vinland Map only muddles an already misty situation. How well do the sagas lend authority to
the map's depiction of Vinland and to its identification as North
America?

Whatever Bjarni and Leif saw, separately or together, was
passed along by them by word of mouth to others, who in their
turn passed the tales of these exploits along, always by word of

mouth, to another generation, and so on until finally they were hearing of a story and the passing of it along to someone else, given written form, several centuries and many generations removed from the doers of the deeds. If the reader is curious to learn what tricks the human memory can play between the even in a matter of great personal importance to the teller, I suggest he visit a courtroom. There, day after day, case after case, will be seen witnesses to the same event, intelligent people attempting to tell the truth, giving the most sharply conflicting testimony dealing with events they saw only a year or two, or at most five or six years, before.

Add to the distortions introduced by the unreliability of human memory and the inadequacy of oral transmission the fact that these tales were passed on as the folk legends of a justifiably proud people, embroidered, as legend by definition must be, with fancies and metamorphoses, and you will arrive at your own conclusions as to the reliability of the sagas as chronicles of fact.

The fact that the sagas survived for centuries through oral transmission attests to their value as entertainment; as history they are no more reliable than the Arabian Nights. They are described by Magnus Magnusson and Hermann Palsson as "a unique blend of entertainment and learning, fact and fantasy, history and storytelling, literary endeavour and family pride, pagan past and Christian present." (*The Vinland Sagas,* Baltimore: Penguin Books, 1965, p. 37)

Nothing I say in these chapters is to be construed as deprecation of the Norse sagas as the epic literature of a people, nor of the accomplishments and character of the people who made these sagas. Nor am I attacking the competence and good faith of the many scholars, a number of whom I quote, who, without misrepresenting the nature of the sagas, base speculations on them frequently at variance with my own thinking. I am simply deploring here the unwarranted assumption on the part of some that historical theories based on these sources are the same as historical fact; I am deploring the attitude that leads them to offer as if proven the pet hypotheses suggested to them by their interpretations of the sagas. The sagas suggest much and prove little. The Vinland Map, if it is genuine at all, diminishes this suggestiveness by offering data in conflict with the sagas.

Pierce G. Fredericks, in his article entitled "Who Discovered America?" in the New York *Times,* October 17, 1965, said that the Norse sagas "in addition to a certain amount of poetic hyperbole, probably suffered a good deal of distortion during the two hundred years they were passed along verbally before anyone wrote them down."

Magnusson and Palsson (op. cit.) say: "It must always be borne in mind that the Icelandic sagas were never museum pieces, embalming for all time a literary act; they were living things, and later generations thought nothing of adapting or rewriting them to suit changing tastes."

Halldor Hermannsson, in his book *The Vinland Sagas* (Ithaca: Cornell University Press, 1944) says of the sagas:

> "The general opinion now is that most of them by far were written in the thirteenth century. That means, that they describe events which happened two or three hundred years earlier, and it naturally raises the question as to reliability of the tradition upon which they are based and about their value as historical sources . . . There was also the faulty memory of many listeners to be reckoned with; they could not remember the story exactly as they had heard it. . . . Story-tellers often may have given a certain twist to a story in order to please, or amuse, their audiences, and sometimes they probably were not above the suspicion of partiality in their presentations."

And greater even than the difficulty of justifying oral tradition as a source for history as opposed to hypothesis, is the difficulty of justifying it as a source for cartography. A map drawn from memory will be a poor enough document; a map drawn from the memory of someone else and passed on through the fallible memories of countless intermediaries, totally useless.

This fact is admitted quite candidly in the Vinland-Tartar book, and reflected in its qualification of the Vinland Map as not embodying "geographical experience."

Many persons speak glibly on the sagas without really knowing them, referring to them as if they were holy writ. Archibald R. Lewis, writing in *Book Week* (December 5, 1965), says of the literature on the Viking voyages to the North American continent: "Much of this literature, because of the confused and contradictory evidence upon which it is based, is unsatisfactory and controversial, so much so that some scholars have dismissed the whole affair as legendary."

In his classic *History of the United States,* the illustrious nineteenth-century historian, George Bancroft, said:

> "The story of the colonization of America by Northmen rests on narratives mythological in form, and obscure in meaning, ancient yet not contemporary. The intrepid mariners who colonized Greenland could easily have extended their voyages to Labrador, and have explored the coasts to the south of it. No clear historic evidence establishes the natural probability that they accomplished the passage, and no vestige of their presence on our continent has been found."

The last clause is still true.

Arthur Middleton Reeves, a Scandinavian scholar of renown, commenting on this passage from Bancroft, says in his book *The Finding of Wineland the Good* (Oxford University Press, 1895) that "if by colonization is meant the permanent settlement or continuous occupation of the country for a long series of years, it should be noted that its story rests on the fertile imagination of comparatively recent editors, not upon the original Icelandic records."

Perhaps there is no better way to express it than in the words of Washington Irving, in his famous life of Christopher Columbus:

"As far as authenticated history extends, nothing was known of terra firma, and the islands of the western hemisphere, until their discovery towards the close of the fifteenth century. A wandering bark may occasionally have lost sight of the landmarks of the old continents, and been driven by tempests across the wilderness of waters long before the invention of the compass, but never returned to reveal the secrets of the ocean. And though, from time to time, some document has floated to the shores of the old world, giving to its wondering inhabitants evidences of land far beyond their watery horizon; yet no one ventured to spread a sail, and seek that land enveloped in mystery and peril. Or if the legends of the Scandinavian voyagers be correct, and their mysterious Vinland was the coast of Labrador, or the shore of Newfoundland, they had but transient glimpses of the new world, leading to no certain or permanent knowledge, and in a little time lost again to mankind. Certain it is that at the beginning of the fifteenth century, when the most intelligent minds were seeking in every direction for the scattered lights of geographical knowledge, a profound ignorance prevailed among the learned as to the western regions of the Atlantic; its vast waters were regarded with awe and wonder, seeming to bound the world as with a chaos, into which conjecture could not penetrate, and enterprise feared to adventure."

What was Vinland and where was it? An Icelandic *Geographical Treatise,* possibly compiled in the twelfth century but preserved only in a manuscript of circa 1300, maintains that Vinland was thought by some to be connected with Africa! No known Norse text refers to it as an island, although that is the way it is drawn on the Vinland Map. Great store is placed by some in a reference to Vinland as an island made about 1075 by one Adam of Bremen, in *Descriptio insularum Aquilonis,* but Adam got his information from King Svein Ulfsson of Denmark, and where King Svein got his from is anybody's guess. Furthermore, Adam, in his geography, placed Vinland *east* of Greenland and Iceland. His description of Vinland, which did not appear in print until 1595, contained this happy note: "Beyond this island, it is said, that there is no habitable land in that ocean, but all those regions which are beyond are filled with insupportable ice and boundless gloom." (Reeves, op. cit., p. 92)

Does this sound like Cape Cod? or Chesapeake Bay? or Florida? For those are among the places that various theorists have advanced as the site of Leif's Vinland. The books which have been written on the Norse sagas are legion, and their differences as to the location of the various landfalls of the Vikings are as varied as the fish in the sea. Edward Reman points out:

> "Many volumes have been written on the discoveries of the Northmen in America in the eleventh century since the Icelander Thormoour Torfaeus published his *History of Vinland* in 1705. For two hundred and forty years historians and students of the sagas have disagreed in their identifications of the various landfalls made by the voyagers to Vinland." (*The Norse Discoveries and Explorations in America*, Berkeley: University of California Press, 1949)

Among the scores of scholars who have attempted to engraft Vinland on the North American continent, we may cite the following: Reman placed Vinland in Hudson Bay; Fernald in Labrador; Ingstad in Newfoundland; Hovgaard in Labrador and Newfoundland; Steensby in the St. Lawrence Estuary; Hermannsson in Baie de Chaleur (south of the Gaspé Peninsula); Thordarson in New Brunswick; Gustav Storm in Nova Scotia; Haugen in southern New England; Fiske in Massachusetts; Rafn in Rhode Island; Gathorne-Hardy in Long Island Sound; Mjelde in Virginia; Reuter in Georgia and Florida.

And still the efforts continue, the latest to reach my attention being *Westviking*, by Farley Mowat, published 1965, by Atlantic Monthly Press, Boston, in which the author, in order to trace the Norse voyages and locate the landfalls, says he "re-arranged" the sagas.

If we owe no other debt to the compilers of the Vinland-Tartar book, we nevertheless should feel grateful to Mr. Skelton for introducing, as a footnote, these words of Mark Twain: "Researches of many commentators have already thrown much darkness on this subject, and it is probable that, if they continue, we shall soon know nothing at all about it."

Chapter 13

A PARAGRAPH HERE, A CONTINENT THERE

There are two saga accounts of the discovery of Vinland by the Norsemen. The *Saga of Eirik the Red* was written in the middle or the latter half of the thirteenth century; it has survived in two manuscripts, of which the older, *Hauksbok*, dates from the early fourteenth century. The *Greenlanders' Saga*, in its oldest surviving form, constituted a part of the *Flatey Book*, a collection of sagas written down in the late fourteenth century, presumably two centuries after the composition of the *Greenlanders' Saga*. All of these manuscripts are Icelandic.

Their divergences in recording the sequence of events of the Norse explorations are profound and various. Most modern students, noting the abundance of discrepancies, absurdities and mythical or supernatural elements in the *Greenlanders' Saga* have tended to discredit it, and to state that where it differs from the *Saga of Eirik,* it must be rejected, and where unconfirmed by the latter, it must be considered doubtful.

An attempt at reconciling the differences between the two tales is made in the Vinland-Tartar book by approving the opinion of William Hovgaard that "different names may have been applied to different lands by different explorers. Thus . . . the Markland of one expedition may have been the Vineland of another, and the Helluland of one expedition may not have been the Helluland of another." (*The Voyages of the Norsemen to America*, New York: The American-Scandinavian Foundation, 1914, p. 221)

It is obvious that accuracy is acutely imperiled when an attempt at reconciling two conflicting stories so that both emerge with full credit is based upon such arbitrary assumptions.

Regarding the two sagas, "both are the workings over of original material in accordance with the well-established facts of saga-making," writes Gwyn Jones, Professor of English Language and Literature at the University College of Wales and past President of the Viking Society for Northern Research, in his book *The Norse Atlantic Saga* (Oxford University Press, 1964). He says further: "Deviations, accretions, influences, reinterpretations, misunderstandings (especially as to the different places reached by the different explorers), changes of emphasis, and varying allocations of credit are to be expected . . ." Theodore M. Andersson in his *The Problem of Icelandic Saga Origins* (New Haven: Yale University Press, 1964) points out that Icelandic oral traditions reside to a great extent in the realm of "speculation and logic", and that available records are silent on "how a saga was told or how it was conferred to parchment."

Let us now consider the *Saga of Eirik the Red,* the one preferred by most of the scholars in the field, the one that is generally regarded as the foundation for the belief that Leif Ericson discovered America. This saga is about 25 book pages long. How much is devoted to the "discovery"?

The saga relates a conversation between Leif Ericson and King Olaf Tryggvason of Norway in which the King asks Leif if he intends to go to Greenland. Leif affirms this, and the King orders Leif to become his Christian missionary in Greenland. There is further polite exchange, during which Leif comments on the difficulty of such a mission, and King Olaf asserts confidence in Leif's luck.

After this introduction comes the paragraph relating the discovery of America. That's right—paragraph. One paragraph, which I quote in its entirety (in quoting from the sagas, I use the texts printed in *The Norse Atlantic Saga,* by Gwyn Jones, Oxford University Press, 1964):

"Leif put to sea as soon as he was ready, was storm-tossed a long time, and lighted on those lands whose

existence he had not so much as dreamt of before.
There were wheatfields growing wild there and vines
too. There were also those trees which are called
maple, and they fetched away with them samples of all
these things. Leif found men on a wreck and carried
them home with him, and provided them all with
lodgings for the winter, showing great magnanimity
and gallantry in this as in so much else, since it was he
who introduced Christianity into the country [Green-
land], besides rescuing these men; and ever afterwards
he was called Leif the Lucky."

This, then, is the vaunted proclamation of the discovery of
America by Leif Ericson! From Norway to North America in a
single sentence! Not only is there nothing which says that Leif's
accidental landfall was North America, there is nothing to indicate the sea over which he was "storm-tossed." It is convenient
for the Vinland champions to take it for granted that the Atlantic Ocean is indicated, but it could just as easily have been the
Norwegian Sea, the Barents Sea, or the North Sea. As for Leif's
being storm-tossed the width of the Atlantic, Samuel Eliot
Morison has said that "it is impossible for a vessel to be 'blown
across' the North Atlantic from east to west. I challenge anyone
to produce a single instance."

No physical description of the land Leif arrived at, no indication of the direction in which Leif was storm-tossed, nor the
length of time. No wonder he is still called Leif the Lucky: on
the basis of one ambiguous paragraph he is credited with discovering a continent . . . but not conceded by everyone.

After Leif's return to Brattahlid, the farm of his father,
Eirik the Red, in Eiriksfjord, Greenland, Leif's brother, Thorstein, decided to "go find this land which Leif had discovered."
He, too, was storm-tossed, but without Leif's luck: his ship
somehow reached Iceland, almost reached Ireland, and wound
up back in Greenland . . . all of this while trying to get to a
place so confidently assumed by the Vinland champions to be
America. Edward Reman, native Norwegian, concludes: "The
fact that Thorstein failed, although he bore the reputation of a

good and prudent man, is sufficient to warn us against ascribing to the Norse voyagers any great knowledge of navigation, or more than human foresight." (Reman, op. cit., p. 116)

I summarize this next incident, not because it has any bearing on the supposed discovery of America, but to give the reader some of the flavor of the sagas, to illustrate the nature of these old tales which have become the gospel of those unwilling to accept the achievement of Columbus.

Thorstein Ericson married Gudrid, then fell ill; so did Sigrid, the wife of another Thorstein, a farmer (called Thorstein the Black in the *Greenlanders' Saga*), and now host to his namesake and bride. Sigrid died, but her corpse showed a remarkable determination:

> ". . . Thorstein Eiriksson sent word to his namesake that he should come and see him, saying that things looked far from healthy there, and that the lady of the house was trying to get on her feet and under the clothes with him. And by the time he arrived back indoors she had worked her way up on to the edge of the bed alongside him. He caught her by the hands and laid a poleaxe to her breast."

Thorstein, Leif's brother, that is, died that same evening. His corpse, not to be outdone by Sigrid's, also rose up, but not to attempt a seduction, merely to have a final talk with Gudrid. Then he finally died.

Another explorer enters the story: Thorfinn Karlsefni, son of Thord Horse-Head. After marrying the widowed Gudrid, Karlsefni, with Snorri Thorbrandsson, "resolved to go and find Vinland." This, by the way, is the first mention by name of Vinland in the text. Here is the story of the next discovery of Vinland (there is of course no indication that Karlsefni reached the same land as Leif):

> "They then sailed away for the Western Settlement and for Bjarneyjar, Bear Isles. From Bjarneyjar they sailed with a north wind, were at sea two days, and

then found land. They rowed ashore in boats and explored the country, finding many flat stones there, so
big that a pair of men could easily clap sole to sole on
them. There were many arctic foxes there. They gave
the land a name, calling it Helluland, Flatstone Land.
Then they sailed with a north wind for two days, when
land lay ahead of them, with a great forest and many
wild animals. Off the land to the south-east lay an island, where they found a bear, so called it Bjarney,
Bear Island. But the land where the forest was they
called Markland, Wood Land.

"Then when two days were past they sighted
land, and sailed to the land. Where they arrived there
was a cape. They beat along the coast and left the land
to starboard; it was an open harbourless coast there,
with long beaches and sands. They put ashore in boats,
came across the keel from a ship, so called the place
Kjalarness, Keelness. Likewise they gave a name to the
beaches, calling them Furdustrandir, Marvelstrands, it
was such a long business sailing past them. Then the
land became bay-indented, and towards these bays they
headed their ships."

While Karlsefni and his crew are cruising the shores of
whatever land they reached, I would like to digress for a moment. Arthur Middleton Reeves points out in his book (op. cit.,
p. 3) that "the eldest surviving manuscript containing an account of the discovery of Wineland the Good, as the southern-
most land reached by the Icelandic discoveries was called, was
written not later than 1334." Since Leif's voyage is said to have
occurred in the year 1000, and Karlsefni's not many years afterward, the present form of the *Saga of Eirik the Red* embodies
well over three centuries' worth of the distortions and accretions of oral transmission plus whatever discrepancies there
were between the first writing of the tale and the surviving
manuscripts. The reliability of word-of-mouth transmission of
a story is notoriously weak. Consider what can happen to a story

over centuries of retelling, and you will have an idea of the trustworthiness of the Icelandic sagas as *history*.

> "Iceland preserved only a fragmentary and inaccurate tradition of the discovery of Vinland. If Icelanders had any knowledge of Bjarni's voyage, it was soon lost; their recollection of Leif's discoveries was so faded as to be worthless." (Reman, op. cit., p. 58) "It is evident that the land or, more probably lands seen by Karlsefni on this cruise are described too loosely to warrant any identification of them. When both the distances and directions given, and the descriptions of land sighted, are so misleading and ambiguous, nothing can be made of them." (Reman, op. cit., p. 169)

William Hovgaard, former Commander in the Royal Danish Navy, says in his book *The Voyages of the Norsemen to America* (op. cit., p. 236):

> "When we try to reconcile the geographical account of Karlsefni's voyage with the conditions actually existing in Nova Scotia and Newfoundland, we soon meet several obvious discrepancies in point of topography and navigation. In fact, it seems impossible to find any solution which tallies completely with the saga."

Getting back to the saga, Karlsefni's company spent the winter on an island at the mouth of a fjord, Straumfjord. In the spring, Thorhall the Hunter, the party's malcontent, decided to search for the elusive Vinland by sailing north again. Taking a splinter crew with him, he did so, but running into strong headwinds, he didn't quite make Vinland; he landed in Ireland! There he died in slavery.

Meanwhile, back at the fjord: Karlsefni and his party sailed south, settling for the next winter at an estuary which they called Hop, but not before they first encountered the Skraelings, "small ill favoured men" with "ugly hair on their heads" who, "astonished," rowed away in their skin boats. The following spring there was a pitched battle with those Skraelings, who were getting distinctly the better of it until Freydis, a woman of the Norse party, took the men to task:

> " 'Why are you running from wretches like these?' she cried. 'Such gallant lads as you, I thought for sure you would have knocked them on the head like cattle. Why, if I had a weapon, I think I could put up a better fight than any of you!' "

Freydis, suiting action to word, entered the battle, although she "was rather slow because of her pregnancy." She picked up the sword of a dead man at her feet, and then:

> "She pulled out her breasts from under her shift and slapped the sword on them, at which the Skraelings took fright, and ran off to their boats and rowed away. Karlsefni's men came up to her, praising her courage."

The next foe the Karlsefni expedition encounters is a uniped. That's right, the same kind of one-legged speed-demon that was described in the Tartar Relation. This emigrant from Uniped Land hopped up to the Norsemen, killed Thorvald, another son of Eirik the Red, with an arrow, and hopped away again, outspeeding his pursuers.

Shortly after this incident, the saga returns Karlsefni to Greenland, and presently to Iceland. We need only mention, in passing, the misfortune of one Bjarni Grimolfsson, whose ship, on the return to Greenland, was blown off course into the Greenland Sea and sunk by worms, a sea full of them, boring holes in the hull. It is strange how the destinies of the pre-Columbian "discoverers" of America are so inextricably bound up with worms.

There are only two other references to Leif himself, the man who, primarily on the evidence of this, the most veracious,

the most trustworthy, of the Norse-"American" sagas, is credited
with the discovery of our continent. Prior to the events related
before, we are told some of the pre-Vinland aspects of Leif's
career, which include being blown off course (again!) while
sailing from Greenland to Norway, this time winding up in the
Hebrides. There he sires an illegitimate son, Thorgils. When
the mother, Thorgunna, while still pregnant, insists on going to
Greenland with Leif, who rejects her plea, appeasing her with a
gift of a gold ring, a woolen cloak, and walrus-ivory belt,
Thorgunna evidently accepts this as adequate compensation for
her interesting condition, for she is not mentioned again. No
wonder he was called Leif the Lucky. But Leif's new son does
eventually get to Greenland, "and there was thought to be
something rather queer about him before the finish."

It is after the Thorgunna idyll that Leif reaches Norway
and is charged by King Olaf with his Christianizing mission.
The only other mention of Leif Ericson in the entire saga is in
the Karlsefni story, where it is pointed out that a pair of Scots, a
man and a woman, in the expedition were originally given to
Leif by King Olaf. Halldor Hermannsson in his *The Problem
of Wineland* (Ithaca, N.Y.: Cornell University Press, 1936)
states that the central figure of the *Saga of Eirik the Red* is not
Leif Ericson but Gudrid. Also that Leif "is little more than a
name to us." (p. 29)

We need not concern ourselves here with the remaining
portions of the *Saga of Eirik the Red,* since they have no connection with the discovery of any lands that might be America.
Suffice to say that this saga is a strange concoction of high adventure (the discovery of Greenland by the outlaw Eirik) related
in a startlingly perfunctory fashion, interlarded with superstition related in an utterly gullible fashion, plus the most trivial
incidents imaginable for an epic tale, related in the most
minutely detailed fashion. For instance, when Thorbjorg, a
seeress, is invited to dinner at the house of a leading farmer,
who hopes she will oblige with some prophecies, a description
of what she wore that evening is given. It would seem to come
right out of a modern society columnist's description of a fancy
wedding, with every detail of the bride's dress. Nor does the

saga-maker deny to his audience any of the facts about what she ate for dinner. At this crucial event in the world's history, Thorbjorg had a porridge made of "goat's bestings," and for meat "the hearts of all living creatures that were available there." Neither are we left in the dark about what utensils she used for eating those delicacies: "a brass spoon and a walrus-ivory-handled knife mounted with a double ring of copper, with its point broken off."

It is unfortunate, for the sake of those who would use the testimony of the sagas to support theories about the discovery of America, that the oral transmitters of these "facts" had just about the same number of words to say about Leif Ericson's finding of Vinland as about what Thorbjorg wore to a dinner party. One paragraph . . . "with its point broken off."

Chapter 14

SOUR GRAPES

According to the *Saga of Eirik the Red,* as told in a single paragraph, Leif Ericson discovered North America, or at least some place called Vinland. According to the *Greenlanders' Saga,* Bjarni Herjolfsson discovered the same place. Let us now examine the latter, so that you may see whether it has any more of the authenticity of history.

Bjarni was the son of Herjolf Herjolfsson, living in Eyrar, Iceland. One year (reputedly 986, although no years are assigned in the sagas) while Bjarni was spending the winter in Norway, his father Herjolf sold his farm and went to live in Greenland at Herjolfsnes. When Bjarni returned to Eyrar and learned his father had sailed away to Greenland, he decided to join him in his new home. He did not know where Greenland was, and he said to his crew: "Our voyage will appear foolhardy, since no one of us has entered the Greenland Sea." They sailed for three days before losing sight of Iceland.

> "Then their following wind died down, and north winds and fogs overtook them, so that they had no idea which way they were going. This continued over many days, but eventually they saw the sun and could then get their bearings (or determine the quarters of the heavens). They now hoisted sail, and sailed that day before sighting land, and debated among themselves what land this could be."

Bjarni said that "to his way of thinking" this "could not be Greenland." Instead of landing, Bjarni sailed his ship close to the shore and "could soon see that the land was not mountainous and was covered with forest, with low hills there, so they left the land to port of them and let their sheet turn towards the land." The lack of conviction on the part of Bjarni and his men as to whether or not the country before them was Greenland, which they had never seen, continued:

> "They sailed for two days before sighting another land. They asked whether Bjarni thought this in its turn was Greenland. In his opinion, he said, this was no more Greenland than the first place—'For there are very big glaciers reported to be in Greenland.'
> "They soon drew near to this land, and could see that it was flat country and covered with woods. Then their following wind died on them."

After a dispute between the crew, who wanted to go ashore for water and wood, and Bjarni, who wanted to keep moving,

> ". . . they turned their prow from the land and sailed out to sea three days with a southwest wind, and then they saw the third land, and this land was high, mountainous, and glaciered. They asked whether Bjarni would put ashore there but no, he said, he had no wish to. 'For to me this land looks good for nothing.' So without so much as lowering their sail they held on along the land, and came to see that it was an island.
> "Once more they turned their prow from the land and held out to sea with the same following wind . . . This time they sailed for four days, and then saw the fourth land. They asked Bjarni whether he thought this was Greenland or not. 'This is very like what I am told about Greenland,' replied Bjarni, 'and here we will make for the land.' "

This place, happily, turns out to be Greenland, but it takes a strong act of faith for an interpreter to be at all sure that the three previous sightings were not also of parts of the very long coastline of Greenland. Sailing without compass or chart to a land they had never seen, sparsely inhabited and only partially explored, Bjarni and his men could hardly have been expected to recognize most Greenland scenery when they saw it. It is significant that when they finally did make their landing, it was right where Bjarni's father lived, with a boat visible on the shore. Halldor Hermannsson in his book *The Problem of Wineland* (op. cit.) finds all this difficult to digest:

> "He [Bjarni Herjolfsson] goes in search of a newly discovered land [Greenland], absolutely unknown to him, is lost in the vast expanse of the North Atlantic, sees one land after the other, dismisses them with the mere waving of the hand, and then lands at the very spot which he is seeking. All this is supposed to have taken place late in the summer, or early in the autumn, when days have become short, generally with the sky overcast, nights long and dark, and weather unfavorable. Such things do not happen in our workaday world, they only happen in fairy tales and lying sagas . . . It is indeed strange that anyone should have given credence to such a story . . ." (pp. 35–36)

Bjarni was invited to Norway by Earl Eirik who appointed him his "retainer" in Greenland. In Norway he "gave an account of those travels of his."

The saga relates that upon Bjarni's return to Greenland from Norway, Leif "bought his ship from him," and then, without a word about the voyage, the direction sailed, or the duration of the trip, the saga at once plunges into landfall:

> "They lighted on that land first which Bjarni and his people had lighted on last. They sailed to land there, cast anchor and put off a boat, then went ashore, and could see no grass there. The background was all

great glaciers, and right up to the glaciers from the sea
as it were a single slab of rock."

Leif named this place Helluland (Slabland). Forgetting,
for the time being, the utter lack of concordance between the
two versions of Leif's journey in the two sagas, what evidence do
we have that Helluland was any part of North America? Listen
to Professor Gustav Storm:

> "When perusing the Grp [*Greenlanders' Saga*] I
> cannot resist the feeling that the record of Grp must
> date from a period when essential parts of the tradition
> had already to a great extent become obfuscated and
> obscure, and hence that, to fill up the gaps, its author
> did not scruple to draw from his own imagination. At
> the outset, it conveys a discordant impression on the
> reader to hear tell respecting Helluland that 'high up
> were prodigious glaciers, but the space from the sea to
> the glaciers was like a continuous slab,' since as is well
> known, there is in North America no country south of
> Greenland with glaciers!" (*Studies on the Vineland
> Voyages,* Copenhagen, 1888)

For that matter, if we accept that the voyages of Bjarni and
Leif were not entirely apocryphal, how do we know that the
place reached by Leif was the same seen by Bjarni? The blasé
Bjarni, discoverer of a continent but too jaded or too timid to
step off his boat, even to take on water after being blown so
many days off course: what a thorn in the side of the intrepid
theorists who cruise the coasts of northeastern North America in
their efforts to make this cape and that bay and the other beach
jibe with the laconic sailing times, directions, and descriptions
given in the sagas. There is something slightly incongruous
about learned men debating among themselves whether
Bjarni's ship, at any given moment, was along the Labrador,
Newfoundland, or Nova Scotia coast.

Leif or Bjarni? (Or both together, if one believes the Vinland Map?) Professor Storm is reported by Reman (op. cit. p.

17) to consider the narrative of Bjarni's voyage absolute fiction, unworthy of serious consideration. At least Leif, in the version of his voyage given in the *Greenlanders' Saga*, shows a decent curiosity about the land he has reached. After setting foot in Helluland, Leif sailed an indeterminate time and reached another land, with woods and beaches, which he called Markland (Forestland). After going ashore again, the party sailed for another two days and reached its third landfall: an island near a headland, and on the shore of the mainland a river mouth. Here Leif spent the winter, anchoring his boat in the lake at the head of the river. There is a favorable description of the climate and the fishing: "No frost came during the winter, and the grass was hardly withered." There is no mention of any encounter with the Indians.

This was the country that Leif named Vinland, and this is the legend of how it was named: One day a German in the party, Tyrkir, returned from a one-man unauthorized exploration trip "rolling his eyes all ways, and pulling faces." He was evidently drunk. At first he could speak only German, but eventually remembered his Icelandic and told Leif: "I have found vines and grapes." And before sailing back to Greenland, Leif and his party gathered grapes, as well as felling timber, for a cargo.

Professor Storm shakes his head at the whole Bjarni Herjolfsson–Leif Ericson story:

> "The long interval between the voyages of Bjarni and of Leiv is left quite unexplained; surely a man in Greenland was in no need of sailing over to Norway and learning what Earl Erik or his courtiers had to tell, to wake a desire of investigating regions possessing so many advantages compared to Greenland."

Storm fires a fusillade of sarcasm:

> "Vineland has so tropical a climate that in winter 'there was no frost, and the grass dried up but little!' Again, the description of grapes and 'wine-trees' in

Vineland is no less singular and evinces a remarkable
want of knowledge concerning wine and grapes. These
grapes are discovered in winter, nay even in spring (!)
The man who finds them gets drunk from eating the
fruit (!) the grapes are gathered, too, in the spring (!)
and the ship's boat filled with them (!) And again, the
vines (vinvior) are spoken of as big trees, felled for
timber (!) Strange to say, a German is made to discover the grapes and this German bears the astonishing name of Tyrker (Turk)!" (op. cit. pp. 323–25)

Is the *Greenlanders' Saga* worthy of entering the outer
lobby of the hall of reliable chronicle? And if it is not, are we to
give Leif Ericson credit for discovering America on the basis of
the one single paragraph in the *Saga of Eirik the Red?*

The next expedition to Vinland, according to the *Greenlanders' Saga,* was undertaken by Leif's brother Thorvald. The
action is a little livelier than on Leif's trip. For one thing, the
keel of Thorvald's ship broke on a cape, which he named
Kjalarness (Keelness). And, unlike Leif, Thorvald ran into the
Skraelings. First, nine of them, of whom the Vikings killed
eight. Then, after a supernatural sleepiness overtook the Norsemen, who could not stay awake, they were suddenly startled by
a cry out of the empty air, obviously in their own language:
" 'Rouse ye, Thorvald, and all your company, if you would stay
alive. Back to your ship with all your men, and leave this land
as fast as you can!' "

Who uttered the cry, how was it that he spoke Icelandic,
and how he knew Thorvald's name are not recorded. The avid-
ity with which some Vinlandophiles interpret literally almost
everything in the sagas is well illustrated by the justification for
this passage offered by Charles Michael Boland: the warning cry
came from an Irish-Icelander-Indian who was already living
nearby in a colony of Irish monks! (*They All Discovered America,* Garden City: Doubleday, 1961, pp. 234–35)

Cry or no cry, the Skraelings attacked, and Thorvald was
killed by an arrow, and was buried at a place he antehumously

named Krossanes. This is the same Thorvald who was killed by the uniped as a member of Karlsefni's expedition. After the party's return, the third Ericson brother, Thorstein, resolved to go to Vinland and fetch his brother's body, but for a whole summer his ship was storm-tossed and ultimately they all landed back in Greenland again. And now, once more, we are treated to the episode of the double deaths of Thorstein, as the guest of the farmer, Thorstein the Black, and the latter's wife, who is here called Grimhild rather than Sigrid. This version is expurgated. After Grimhild's death, Thorstein Ericson, ill himself, spoke:

> " 'Marvelous are the ways of our hostess now, for she is heaving herself up on her elbows, and swinging her feet over the bedstock, and feeling for her shoes.' At that same moment in came franklin Thorstein, and instantly Grimhild lay down, and every beam in the room gave out a groan."

No seduction this time: Grimhild/Sigrid is satisfied to reach for her shoes. Thorstein Ericson died, and again his corpse sat up and engaged in a colloquy with his wife Gudrid.

The *Greenlanders' Saga* also tells the story of the Karlsefni expedition but with so many differences from the one related in the *Saga of Eirik the Red* that it could never be regarded as its twin brother. In the *Eirik the Red Saga*, Karlsefni named the lands he sighted as Helluland, Markland and Keelness. But in the Greenlanders' narrative, Karlsefni did no naming; he immediately went ashore from his ship and cut up a stranded whale to feed himself and his crew of sixty men and five women. He then landed from his ship "all sorts of livestock." It is difficult to visualize a trim, deckless Viking ship carrying sixty-six persons and a cargo of cattle. One bull "began to bellow and bawl his head off," frightening the Skraelings who ran away. Since Karlsefni intended to trade with the natives, he had to gain their good will, and he did this by offering them milk from his cows. How many cows voyaged in that tight Viking boat that Karlsefni could satisfy the hordes of hungry savages by giving them milk in exchange for their "bales of grey furs and sables and skins of all kinds"?

It would be inevitable that the Greenlanders' tale would deal with supernatural events such as constantly erode the sagas' claims as true records of history. Gudrid, Thorstein's widow, and now married to Karlsefni, was sitting inside the doorway—

> "when a shadow fell across the door and a woman walked indoors in a dark close-fitting kirtle—rather short she was, and wearing a band around her head, her hair a light chestnut, pale of face, and with such big eyes that no one ever saw their equal in a human skull. She walked to where Gudrid was sitting.
>
> " 'What is your name?' she asked.
>
> " 'My name is Gudrid. And what is your name?'
>
> " 'My name is Gudrid,' she replied.
>
> "At that Gudrid the housewife held out her hand to her, that she should sit down beside her, when all of a sudden Gudrid heard a loud crash and the woman disappeared."

The next and last voyage to Vinland recorded in this saga was a strictly commercial enterprise, in which equal shares were held by two brothers, Helgi and Finnbogi, and Freydis, the same half-sister of Leif, Thorvald and Thorstein who routed the Skraelings in so remarkable a fashion in the *Saga of Eirik's* account of Karlsefni's expedition.

In the *Greenlanders' Saga* Freydis, after arriving at Leif's original settlement in Vinland, outfaced Helgi and Finnbogi, first wresting possession from them of the house that Leif had built, then cajoling Finnbogi into exchanging the brothers' large ship for her smaller one. Finally, falsely claiming that she had been maltreated by the brothers, she taunted her husband into leading their retainers against the brothers and their followers (Freydis had had the foresight, before leaving Greenland, to sneak an extra five men aboard her ship to outnumber the brothers' forces). Helgi and Finnbogi and their thirty followers were seized in their house, bound, and led outside, one at a time, where "Freydis had each man killed as he came out." There were also five women in the party, whom the men were unwilling to slay, but the ineffable Freydis, exclaiming "hand me an axe," did the job herself.

After Freydis and her husband returned with a rich cargo to Greenland, Leif learned of her atrocities, but forebore punishing his half-sister, contenting himself with a dire prophecy: "I predict this of her and her husband: No offspring of theirs will come to much good."

The remainder of this saga does not deal with any possible North American voyages. The last sentence of the *Greenlanders' Saga* reads:

"And it is Karlsefni who of all men reported most succinctly what happened on all these voyages of which some account has now been given."

But if the saga seems unsatisfactory as history, do not blame poor Karlsefni. Who knows what changes were made in his story before it was finally written down in its present form, more than three and a half centuries later? Who knows whether Bjarni got here first or Leif? Or neither? Who knows whether Thorvald was killed by a uniped on Karlsefni's voyage or by a Skraeling on his own?

Who knows where Vinland was?

Who knows if there ever was a Vinland?

Chapter 15

RUINS AND RUNES

The evidence that Scandinavian mariners were the first
Europeans to land on American soil, five centuries before Christopher Columbus, is twofold: documentary and archaeological,
words and objects.

The documentary evidence—the words—consists of a few
scattered references, and two relatively short narratives, the two
sagas that were discussed in the preceding two chapters. In them
stories are related, totally at variance between one saga and the
other, of the discovery and extremely perfunctory exploration
of places called Vinland, Helluland, Markland, etc. Nowhere
are we given sailing directions so precise, or descriptions of the
lands so detailed and unambiguous, that it is possible to say
"This *has* to be North America." Whatever ingenious, enter-
taining, but purely speculative research is brought to bear on
the problem of identifying the Vikings' possible landfalls on the
basis of the partial, ambiguous and contradictory clues in the
sagas, is drastically vitiated in its usefulness by the distortions
and fictional elements that certainly crept into the sagas during
the centuries of their survival only by word of mouth.

The sagas are tales, not documents. There is no way of
separating the fiction from whatever fact may be reflected in
them except by external evidence—documentary or archaeological—that can prove one, or disprove another, episode. The
principal document that has been brought forward to confirm
the saga stories is the Vinland Map, but its value is nil on three
grounds: 1) the extremely dubious genuineness of the map it-

self; 2) its conjunction of Bjarni and Leif, disputing both sagas; and 3) the overwhelming probability that, even if genuine, the mapmaker was simply drawing "Vinland" out of his imagination to illustrate his own familiarity with the sagas. In other words, the map might be a result of the sagas, not a confirmation of them.

A further qualification of the sagas' usefulness as historical source material is this: if, by some miracle, we could have before us the words of one of the sagas as it was first told, perhaps by a participant in the action, free of transformations, confusions and supernaturalisms, it might still be false! Edward Reman (op. cit., p. 161) suggests:

> "Perhaps to save their pride, they [Karlsefni and his crew] reported, when they reached Greenland, that they had actually succeeded in finding and settling Vinland; the tales of grapes and self-sown wheat, and of a snowless winter, may have been told to give verisimilitude to a face-saving lie."

Those who insist on torturing the saga narratives into chronologies of unassailable history must discard the obvious absurdities of superstition, but in retaining the rest of the episodes they have no greater assurance that these too are not fictional. In choosing, as they must, between two irreconcilable stories—was Bjarni first or Leif? was Thorvald the leader or Karlsefni?—they cannot show why, if the rejected version is false, the accepted one cannot equally be false. And where they prefer, as most of them do, the *Saga of Eirik the Red* to the *Greenlanders' Saga*, they must be content with a single paragraph on the discovery of America. They must also discount the reservations about the reliability of the sagas as historical material of many of the most distinguished scholars in the field—a number of them Scandinavians themselves, many of them believing that Norse seamen reached our shores, but not permitting their beliefs to sabotage their intellectual honesty and precision.

I cite below several more observations from Reman's *The Norse Discoveries and Explorations in America:*

"The text contains no sailing directions whatso-
ever. When it expresses distances sailed at all, it does
so in terms of elapsed time; often even this is not
stated. Scholars who have assumed that sailing distances can be inferred with any closeness from elapsed
time have often unconsciously interpreted such distances in terms of preconceived theory with respect to
the lands discovered." (p. 61)

(Taking the text too literally) "has led investiga-
tors to shuffle possible Marklands all about the Atlantic map in order to find a site compatible with the description of the saga and within two days' sail of Vinland. (p. 69)

"When the text gives directions and sailing distances at all, landfalls which match its descriptions
simply do not lie in those directions or at those approximate distances." (p. 130)

Regarding the ascription of theories of distances covered to the
mentions in the sagas of elapsed time, a further difficulty has
been pointed out by several commentators: the use in the sagas
of the term *doegr* (days). Magnusson and Palsson say:

". . . this term is ambiguous. Strictly speaking,
it means 'day' in the sense of twelve hours, but it is
also used in the sense of the astronomical 'day' of
twenty-four hours, and there is often doubt about the
particular meaning in many early texts." (op. cit., p.
53)

Some readers have seen in the Skraelings (a derogatory
term, by the way), and their use of skin-boats when attacking
the Vikings in the *Greenlanders' Saga*, an obvious reference to
the American Indians. But Commander Hovgaard points out:
"It seems more probable that the statement about skin-boats
crept into the sagas much later, when the saga-writers knew that
the Skraelings in Greenland used boats of this material . . .
and may have inserted comments to that effect in the sagas, in

order to make them more remarkable and interesting."

Similarly, Halldor Hermannsson, unsure even of the existence of Bjarni Herjolfsson, states that the lands which Bjarni saw "must consequently have been invented after these lands had become known in popular tradition." (*The Problem of Wineland,* op. cit., p. 36)

Ex post facto history! Hermannsson feels that "in trying to find a solution of the problem of Wineland, we need pay very little, if any, attention to the *Tale of the Greenlanders.*" (op. cit., p. 47)

Is the *Saga of Eirik* any more authentic? Of it, Mr. Hermannsson says: "Who the author was and where he lived and wrote we cannot tell." It cannot escape the attention of the reader that commentators on the sagas speak of the writers of the sagas as "authors" and not as historians.

There are, as was mentioned at the beginning of this chapter, two ways of substantiating the legends of the Norse discovery of America: words and objects. The words fight among themselves, leaving unscathed the record of Columbus. Do the objects fare better?

The history of the digging up and publicizing of alleged Norse artifacts on American soil is a long, frequently scabrous one. Charlatan and misguided scholar alike have pointed to objects *in situ* or placed them on museum shelves, proclaiming them the detritus of Norse settlement. Here the lunatic fringe of historical romancers has its field day, sometimes providing unintentional amusement, sometimes creating confusion in the academic world.

The most recently well-publicized archaeological find is of what is purported to be a Norse site at L'Anse aux Meadows, Newfoundland. This was excavated by Dr. Helge Ingstad, formerly governor of East Greenland and Spitzbergen, and his archaeologist wife. Intending no disrespect to Dr. Ingstad, whose good faith cannot be doubted, one must be doubly wary of accepting the archaeological evidence which supports the preconceived theory of its finder. Dr. Ingstad expected to find a Norse settlement in Newfoundland, from his interpretation of the sagas; he feels he has found it. But Samuel Eliot Morison, commenting on this latest find in his monumental *Oxford History of the American People* (New York: Oxford University Press, 1965, p. 20), writes:

"... in 1962 a Norwegian archaeologist excavated a site . . . which by carbon dating he believes to have been constructed around the year 1000, and where he thinks he has found the ruins of Leif's house. Possibly authentic Norse remains will be found there; but the evidence so far produced indicates that the site was used for smelting iron by early French colonists."

Radiocarbon dating of organic material, by the way, is very useful for determining the approximate age of prehistoric discoveries, but is still too experimental and imprecise to date material from comparatively recent centuries with sufficient exactitude.

The article in the *National Geographic Magazine* for November, 1964 in which Dr. Ingstad announced his findings is accompanied by a photograph of what appears to be a metallic doughnut. According to the editor's caption, it is

"A soapstone spindle whorl . . . indicating Viking settlers there included women. Unquestionably Norse, the small weight acted as a flywheel, spinning a wooden shaft to twist raw wool into yarn. The implement, of a type common at Norse sites in Greenland, Iceland, and Norway, was fashioned from a fragment of a charred cooking pot."

While one may commiserate with the archaeologist over the sparseness of the clues he frequently has to work with, this seems to be an enormous burden of supposition to impose upon a tiny, nearly featureless object.

Lest the reader, if he has not read Dr. Ingstad's account, visualize the archaeologists walking into a structure, blowing the dust off a Viking helmet, stooping to pick up the "soapstone spindle whorl" and then noticing the "charred cooking pot" with a fragment broken off, here are Dr. Ingstad's words:

"Visible clues to these momentous finds were scanty indeed. Some house sites revealed themselves simply as faint outlines in the turf; others showed not at all at the surface. We scraped in vain for domestic artifacts, such as the spinning weights and the bone and ivory chessmen and other games pieces found widely in Greenland."

Such equivocal clues as a "queer hollow in a sandbank close to the brook" and slag that "looked like the refuse from iron smelting" lead Dr. Ingstad into this reverie:

"My feet pressed the earthen floor where a Viking blacksmith stood to swing his hammer as he forged knives and nails and sword blades."

The theory that led Dr. Ingstad to scour Newfoundland for something that might turn out to be the remains of Vinland was an etymological one. Vinland, Wineland, was named for Leif Ericson's grapes. Wild grapes are not known to have grown anywhere north of Passamaquoddy Bay, on the Maine-Canada border. This would preclude Newfoundland as the site of Vinland, but Dr. Ingstad writes, in the *National Geographic:*

"Although the sagas, partly by allusion to short sailing routes to America, indicate that Vinland was a northern place, most scholars have believed that *vin* referred to wild grapes; thus they have placed Vinland rather far south on the Atlantic coast: near Boston, on Cape Cod, Martha's Vineyard, or Long Island, among many sites. I saw it differently. I came to share with Swedish philologist Sven Soderberg the conviction that 'vin' in Vinland had nothing to do with grapes, but instead was used in the old Norse sense of 'grass' or 'grazing lands.' "

But this view has found only limited acceptance. Magnusson and Palsson (op. cit., p. 58) declare that "On phonological grounds this suggestion is nonsensical, since the name Vinland has never been forgotten in Iceland, and the words . . . are never confused." They go on to point out the specific association of the name Vinland with wine in the sagas.

And so the confusion mounts, with even the very meaning of the name Vinland now in dispute. This should not be surprising, since every new effort to identify the Vikings' landfalls, every new would-be revelation of Norse ruins or relics in America, requires a new interpretation of the meager saga material for justification.

I do not presume to divine whether this Newfoundland site will ever receive the full endorsement of those qualified to pass judgment by expert knowledge coupled with disinterestedness. But it is worth observing that the importance that some have attached to the verification of these traces of some sort of old habitation is the hope of baseball fans that the home team, trailing in the ninth inning by ten runs, may still win. All alleged Norse ruins and leavings up to this time have been annihilatingly rejected by those competent to judge. L'Anse aux Meadows is the only hope left for now . . . except for those diehards who refuse to face the facts about their favorite "finds."

I am happy to observe that the editors of the Vinland-Tartar book, with so much at stake in the acceptance of the Norse discovery of America, are too sophisticated and intellectually honest to be deceived by any of these "genuine finds":

> "Such finds sometimes show a suspicious correlation with areas of nineteenth-century Scandinavian immigration, and genuine medieval ironware may well have been brought from Scandinavia and planted in modern times. The so-called 'small halberds' are known to have been manufactured in the 1890's for cutting plug tobacco!"

The Kensington Rune Stone is probably the most notorious of all these pieces of Scandiknavery. In November, 1898, a farmer, Olaf Ohman, reported that he had turned up on his land, near Kensington, Minnesota, a flat stone incised with a runic inscription. (Runes are the symbols of the ancient Teutonic alphabet.) As deciphered by the stone's principal champion, Hjalmar R. Holand, the runes read:

"8 Goths and 22 Norwegians on explorations journey from Vinland round about the west. We had camp by 2 skerries one day's journey north from this stone. We were and fished one day. After we came home found ten of our men red with blood and dead. AVM save from evil. have ten men by the sea to look after our ships 14 days-journeys from this island. year 1362."

The experts at the University of Oslo, Norway, who could hardly be accused of having ethnic partisanship *against* the Norsemen, declared the inscription to be a "silly, meaningless forgery." When the numerous errors in the inscription were spelled out to Holand, he accounted for them, he thought, by claiming that the carver was "working under tension." One does not have to be an expert in runic inscriptions to recognize the absurdity of the Kensington Stone. If the carver was working so quickly, why did he put in the trivial detail about the fishing trip? And why did he find it necessary to add the literary flourish about the ten dead men being "red with blood?" And how did these pioneers manage to get from Vinland, on the Atlantic seaboard, overland to an island in a vanished lake in Minnesota, half a continent away, in only fourteen days? And what were Scandinavians doing in America at all in 1362? Even the Vinland champions admit that the alleged settlements must have been long abandoned by that date. And finally, just who was supposed to read the runes? Indians? Mr. Ohman, the farmer?

The Kensington Stone once caused quite a flurry in scholarly circles; it could even be called the Vinland Map of its day. (When it was recently exhibited at the Minnesota Pavilion at the New York World's Fair, it received scant attention.)

A stone at Dighton, Massachusetts, was also offered as bearing a runic message indicating a visitation by Scandinavians. It was proved that the inscription had been carved by Indians.

A stone tower in Newport, Rhode Island, has for long been held by theorists to be a Viking construction, even though documentary evidence has conclusively proven it to have been built as a windmill in 1675 by Governor Benedict Arnold (not the Revolutionary War traitor) of Rhode Island.

Edward Reman summarizes the "ruins and runes" situation as follows:

"An inscription found on the shore of No Man's Land, an island off Martha's Vineyard, will serve as an illustration of the blatant forgeries which have been perpetrated in unscrupulous efforts to demonstrate that Leif Eiriksson, or other Norsemen, landed in one or another specific area. The No Man's Land stone contains four lines of runic letters: the first line is taken up by the name LEIF ERIKSSON; the second consists of the date 1001 in Roman letters (MI); the third and fourth are unreadable, although the first three letters in the third line suggest that the carver intended to engrave the name VINLAND. It has been proved that this inscription was made in the nineteenth century, by some man whose knowledge of the runic alphabet was extremely defective.

"Other 'relics' alleged to be Norse have been found from the Atlantic coast westward as far as Minnesota. Some of these are undoubtedly Indian, other American colonial or postcolonial; some are genuine, but not Norse; others are neither Norse nor genuine. Not one single object has ever been found on American soil which the voyagers of the eleventh century can possibly have made or left behind them." (op. cit., pp. 194–95)

Hermannsson reaches the same conclusion: "So far nothing has been found on the American continent which corroborates the information in the literary sources, or gives us any clue as to the places mentioned in them."

And so does Morison: "All alleged relics hitherto 'discovered' were either built centuries later, such as the stone tower at Newport, or are forgeries such as the 'Kensington Rune Stone' and the 'Beardmore Weapons', inscribed or planted by practical jokers."

Where people settle, they leave traces for future archaeologists to find. No undisputed trace of any Norse settlement in North America has yet been found. Perhaps this absence of clues is itself the most eloquent of clues.

Whichever one may choose on the basis of the Icelandic sagas as the discoverer of America, Bjarni or Leif, the most that can be said for them is that they made accidental landfalls somewhere other than their destination. Did Leif and Bjarni, singly or in company, or either one of them, ever sight American shores? I do not know, but I feel that I am well within the bounds of reasonableness when I assert that those who answer that question with an unqualified affirmative cannot show proofs—documentary or archaeological—to justify such a stand.

The fact of the epochal discovery of Christopher Columbus does not need to be pruned of unipeds and walking corpses, buttressed by forged inscriptions and misinterpreted ruins, sifted from the ashes of immolation by distortion. Instead we have accounts written at the time of the occurrences they describe, diaries and journals contemporaneous with the events they relate, histories prepared during or immediately after the unfolding of the drama. We have the history of the discovery of America written by Columbus' own son Ferdinand, who accompanied his father on the fourth voyage; the History of the Indies by Bartolome de las Casas, who worked from Columbus' original papers; the account of the discovery written by Peter Martyr, who began his researches in 1494, knew Columbus personally and was the first person to use the phrase "New World"; and the superb work by Gonzalo de Oviedo, who also knew Columbus, was thoroughly familiar with navigation, and lived for thirty-four years in the Caribbean. And over and above this

mass of first-hand or near-first-hand material, one can study letters written by Columbus, the books which he read with their
marginal notations in his own handwriting, and the official documents anticipating and following the great discovery.

To read these is to feel history.

Part III

COLUMBUS

Chapter 16

"EVERYTHING IN ITS RIGHT PLACE"

We call Christopher Columbus the discoverer of America because, until he crossed the Atlantic Ocean, the American continents had never appeared on a map. No one in Europe knew they were there.

It is therefore shocking how little of the story of Columbus, so well documented both by himself and contemporary writers, appears in our history books. Many people are aware of little more than the names of the three vessels of his first voyage to this hemisphere, the epochal date 1492, and that he was an Italian sailing in the service of King Ferdinand and Queen Isabella of Spain. They may also be burdened with one or more popular misconceptions: that Columbus never set foot on the mainland of the American continents; that the *only* intent of his First Voyage was to find a route to India; and even, astonishingly, that Columbus Day, October 12, is his birthday.

Fortunately, most people have a general awareness of the amazing courage and persistence displayed by this man, both in obtaining the backing for his wonderful enterprise, and in carrying it through against the threats of mutiny and nature. Hero worship may be temporarily out of style, but heroes are immortal; and even among the handful of authentic heroes in our history Columbus stands in the forefront because of his unique combination of attributes. He was the dreamer, the mystic, the visionary, but he was also the man of action, the doer, the architect of a hemisphere. He turned theory into continents, hopes into history.

The true story of Columbus more than confirms this image: it enhances his stature far beyond the ability of any latter-day detractors to diminish. He was not a gold-braided armchair admiral of hereditary fortune, but a self-made man of the sea. He knew all about ships, their seaworthiness, draft, buoyancy and volume, their rigging and rudders, and he knew all about sailing, about tides, wind currents and ocean currents. It was his observation of Atlantic winds, in fact, that made him choose the superbly apt sailing route that led him to his goal, when the blind stabs into the unknown sea that others made would have led to defeat, possibly disaster. He knew the vagaries of nature, the variations of the compass, the signposts of the stars, the geography of the known world . . . and he dedicated his life to unfolding the geography of the unknown world.

Columbus was certainly not the lonely, uncommunicative genius, the solitary eccentric brushed by intuitive greatness; on the contrary, he had to be at home in the world of royal courts and committees and convince them of the soundness of his plans; he had determinedly to pursue his long nourished project in order to obtain the influential friends, financing and moral support he needed for his enterprise.

Cristoforo Colombo was born in Genoa sometime during the late summer or early autumn of 1451, the now generally accepted year. In the fifteenth century Italy was not a nation but rather a geographical expression—a peninsula full of small, jealous city-states. This fact was to cause Columbus in later years to seek from four foreign countries support for his daring project, and finally to sail under the colors of Spain. However, he never surrendered his Genoese citizenship. In a letter to the Bank of St. George of Genoa dated April 2, 1502, he refers to his native city with longing.

The one-time wealth and influence of his forebears, who originally ranked among the most illustrious nobility of Piacenza, had been dissipated by the misfortunes of the wars of Lombardy during which their estates were lost. Christopher's father, who was engaged in the craft of wool weaving, was Domenico Colombo, his mother the former Susanna Fontanarossa.

There were two younger brothers, Bartholomew and Diego, and a sister Bianchinetta. Bartholomew was destined to become Christopher's right arm in the years of trial that lay ahead. Both Bartholomew and Diego, as well as a cousin, Giannetto, were to accompany the navigator to the New World. Family ties, as well as the bonds of friendship and gratitude, loomed large in Christopher's life.

Estimates of Christopher's education range from the claim in the biography written by his son Ferdinand that he attended the University of Pavia, to the claim that he could not read or write until he reached Lisbon at about the age of twenty-four. In regard to the former, scholars feel that Pavia, a small district near Genoa, became confused with the University of Pavia. At any rate, he seems to have received little formal education, but there is no doubt that he was a well-educated man in the true sense of the term. He learned by sailing, by observing, by reading, by talking with authorities in the subjects he loved, and by taking copious notes. For correspondence he wrote in Latin and Spanish. In a letter he addressed to the King and Queen of Spain, he said:

> "To this my wish [that of finding out the secrets of the world] I found our Lord most propitious, and to this end I received from Him a spirit of intelligence. In seamanship He made me abundant, of astrology [including astronomy] He gave me enough, as well as of geometry and arithmetic, and of ingenuity in mind and hands to draw this sphere and on it the cities, rivers and mountains, islands, and harbours, everything in its right place. In this time I have seen and studied all writings, cosmography, histories, chronicles and philosophy and other arts." (*Christopher Columbus,* by Salvador de Madariaga, New York: Macmillan Co., 1940, p. 45)

He read the opinions of the ancients, whose storehouse of scientific achievement fell into such neglect until the dawn of the Renaissance: Aristotle, Strabo, Ptolemy. And of later men seeking to expand anew the boundaries of knowledge: Marco Polo, who alerted Europeans to the potentialities of the Far East; Pierre d'Ailly, whose Imago Mundi can still be seen in a copy with marginal notations in Columbus' hand; and Paolo Toscanelli, the physician of Florence, from whom Columbus received correspondence encouraging him in his geographical views.

In 1479 Columbus wrote that he "became a navigator at the age of 14 and always followed the sea." His early voyages were in the Mediterranean, and were probably interspersed with periods of helping out in the family wool business. In 1476 a Genoese convoy in which he had sailed was attacked by a French fleet; Columbus' ship went down, but he managed to swim ashore. The shore was the southern coast of Portugal, and from there Columbus soon made his way to the maritime center of the world, Lisbon.

Portugal, at the intersection of the two great oceanic highways, the eastern Atlantic and the Mediterranean, was in the vanguard of all Europe in the search for new sea routes to the riches of the East. The fall of Constantinople to the Ottoman Turks in 1453 had effectively sealed the fate of whatever ambitions European merchants might have had to establish a practicable land route to the Orient. The gold and silver, jewels and spices, silks and scents of the Far East now only trickled into European markets, many middlemen removed from their source. Inspired by their outward-looking Prince Henry the Navigator in the mid-fifteenth century, Portuguese seamen searched for the route to Asia around Africa. Farther and farther down the west coast of Africa crept successive expeditions, some leaving trading stations behind them, but no one knew how far south the dark continent extended.

This was the ferment in which the twenty-four-year-old Christopher Columbus found himself in the city of Lisbon. Here he was happy to meet up with his younger brother Bartholomew who by coincidence at that time was living in Lisbon and working for a chart-making firm which supplied maps for mariners. It was perhaps inevitable that the two brothers should form a commercial chart-making enterprise of their own. Then, too, when Columbus married Dona Felipa Perestrello e Moniz in 1479, he came into an inheritance of the charts and sailing records of her late father, Bartholomew Perestrello, who was a noted mariner and had served as a captain in the navy of Prince Henry of Portugal and had been the first governor of Porto Santo in the Madeiras. It was to the Madeiras that the young Columbus took his wife, first to Porto Santo where their only son Diego was born, and then to Funchal. During this period Christopher Columbus was not only increasing his knowledge of the theoretical side of navigation and geography, but he was also sailing on Portuguese ships to the corners of the then accessible world, constantly raising his status in the merchant marine. To the north he reached Galway in Ireland, even sailing as far as 73 degrees North Latitude, well north of Iceland; to the south, on the first ship he commanded, he reached the fortified Portuguese trading post on the Gold Coast of Africa; to the west, he went to the Azores, last stepping-stone to oblivion in the sea-lore of the day.

It has been proposed that, on his voyage to Iceland in 1477, Columbus may have been exposed to information about "Vinland," perhaps through Bristol seamen. This simply cannot be true. No document can be adduced to show that among the sea-going people of Bristol or anywhere else there circulated, at that time, any information about a continent to the west. It is impossible to believe that, with such valuable information at their disposal, no voyagers of northern European countries would have set out to rediscover this land of grapes and "self-sown wheat" until, inspired by the discovery of Columbus, England in 1497 sent the Italian, Giovanni Caboto (John Cabot) westward to the "Indies." And the thoughts, plans, theories and hopes of Columbus, so well documented, would certainly have contained a reference to such a place as Vinland if it had already been discovered.

For these thoughts, plans, theories and hopes were now crystallizing in Columbus' mind. During his years as a Portuguese mariner and chart-maker he was becoming ever more sensitive to the magnetic pull of what lay over the western horizon. Sailing into the world of the setting sun had become the consuming motive of his life. He was convinced that by sailing westward he could reach the Indies, the term generally applied to India, China and Japan (the Cathay and Cipangu of Marco Polo), and the adjacent lands and islands. His motives for discovery were three:

1) Religious, for Columbus was an extremely devout man, and the opportunity of bringing the Gospel to new lands, of Christianizing the unbelievers, exerted a powerful influence on Columbus. He hoped to contact the legendary Prester John in the east so that Europe might join forces with this Christian prince and, attacking from both east and west, drive the infidels once and for all out of the Holy Land.

2) Intellectual, for in so universal and eager a mind as that of Columbus there could have been no greater desire than to complete the picture of the earth, to show the globe finally to all men with "everything in its right place."

3) Commercial, to pump the blood of oriental luxuries through the arteries of European commerce. And if the demands made by Columbus for his personal enrichment may have seemed excessive to some of the sovereigns before whom he laid his plans, today we account them a tiny price for the gift of a hemisphere. And Columbus stood to gain nothing—except a watery death—if there were no land where he looked for it.

How did Columbus know where to seek for land? His vast knowledge and wide experience in navigation were fortunately assisted by a coincidence of errors. Since there was no Vinland Map or prototype floating around the scholarly precincts of Europe, all geographical conceptions had to be erroneous. There was no doubt but that the earth was a sphere, and that, therefore, it was theoretically possible to reach the East by sailing west. What was in dispute was the feasibility of this idea.

Most of the savants thought the ocean separating Europe from Asia far too wide to permit such a voyage. Columbus underestimated the size of the globe by underestimating the number of miles to a degree; further, in company with a minority of others, he added to Ptolemy's overestimate of the extension of Asia the estimated areas of Marco Polo's Cathay and Cipangu. This brought the distance between Japan and the Canary Islands, in Columbus' calculation, to about 2400 nautical miles, less than one-quarter of the actual distance. He also supposed that there were islands along the way. This sanguine estimate of the distance between Europe and Japan by sea was not unique to Columbus, it was shared by the maps of Andrea Bianco and the globe of Martin Behaim.

But where, in the mutual ignorance about the existence of America, the estimate of some of the geographers of the size of the earth was more nearly true than Columbus', it was by being the only one to put his theory to the ultimate test of a voyage of discovery that Columbus made it possible for the truth to become known. By wrongly supposing that some ten thousand miles of uninterrupted sea lay west of Europe, the sages erected a blockade of fear to contain the venturings of European sailors within the limits of the Azores; by correctly supposing that there was land within sailing distance of Europe, although not knowing the true nature of the land, Columbus was able to keep his promises to his sponsoring Spanish sovereigns.

More than theoretical reasoning stiffened Columbus' resolve. His extraordinary competence with a mariner's compass and dividers, quadrant and lead line, reinforced by an intuitive feel of "the way of a ship in the midst of the sea," enabled him to fix his latitude with amazing accuracy and cut the umbilical cord of disorientation that tied so many mariners of the day to within sight or certainty of the coasts. Intriguing clues to the presence of great lands to the west washed up on the beaches of Europe and its satellite islands, and these too stirred the imagination of Columbus. Plants and tree trunks that grew nowhere in the Old World, great canes with joints big enough to hold a gallon of water, oddly wrought pieces of wood that followed long-blowing westerly winds, such as the one seen by Columbus' brother-in-law in Porto Santo: all of these mingled their siren song with the murmur of the waves they rode to catch at the ear of an already westward-yearning seaman.

The suggestion is untenable that Columbus was fortified with some Vinland Map prototype or other indication of a previous discovery of a western continent. Against it are several obvious truths. First, it was always Columbus' stated proposal to reach the riches of the Far East, particularly Japan, and nothing less than the prospect of attaining a shorter route to this known wealth could have secured for him so much as an audience with any European monarch. Then there is Columbus' sailing plan: west from the Canaries, far south of any land responsibly suggested as having been reached by any predecessor. Finally, if Columbus had such a map or tidings of a successful westward voyage, he could have offered it in proof and spared himself many years of disappointment, rejection, humiliation and frustration. As Salvador de Madariaga expresses it in his excellent biography of Columbus:

> "What was Columbus' chief obstacle before statesmen and cosmographers? His lack of documentary proofs. He was heard by virtue of his 'grace', of his magnetic power. But a proof, a document, a map?"

The exhibits that Columbus could offer—such as his chart and letter from Dr. Toscanelli—and his own arguments, were based on deductions from his studies that were out of harmony with the chorus of prevailing opinion. It was with these deductions, and the enormous conviction with which he held to them, that Columbus sought the financial support for his great project.

Chapter 17

"TIERRA!"

The opportunity to sail westward was open to any nation. There was no secret about Columbus' project. It cannot be said that he stole a march on his contemporaries, planning surreptitiously a voyage which others would have attempted had they thought of it. The wisest scientists, the wealthiest monarchs, the most experienced sea captains had reflected on Columbus' enterprise and had vetoed it. It was impossible, they said—unanimously. To begin with, even if a westward voyager could reach a distant land, what assurance was there he could get back? How far away would that land be? And then there were the elements to consider—an always possible violent storm could sink a ship in the twinkling of an eye, with no availability for rescue. No one knew what lay over the horizon; only Columbus ventured to find out; only Columbus dared to test the dire predictions voiced by the most learned and the most unlearned of the day.

The geographers and men of education knew that the earth was round, but there was no proof that, once embarked in any direction, one could return to the starting point, because no one knew what intervened. Commission after commission rejected Columbus' voyage because it was too brimful of risk, too lacking in reasonable hope of success.

Columbus expostulated with the commissions and the royal experts. The sea was a joiner, he argued, not a separator. Some of the wise men accepted this outpouring of sensible talk, but they would ask, how far away is Asia? how far away is India? And Columbus would tell them. He was wrong in his measurements, but he was dead right in his plan, right in his rationalization, right in his monumental conclusions.

How long did Columbus reason with his opponents? How many years did Columbus battle against ignorance, arrogance and outright hostility? It was circa 1480, after an exchange of correspondence with Paolo Toscanelli, the Florentine physician and astronomer, who said that a westward voyage to the Indies was perfectly feasible, that Columbus firmly conceived the idea of his daring enterprise. Twelve years thus were to pass at the dockyards of official hostility and procrastination before his ship of discovery could be launched into the sea toward the setting sun.

Leif Ericson discovered America easily. He got into a long boat in Norway, lightning struck, the winds blew, the sea rose, and before he knew it he had landed in America (or was it Greenland?). But Columbus could not call on the winds of fable and legend, his motive power was argument, scientific deduction, the gathering of further evidence, and the seeking of friendly ears and hope for understanding hearts—for twelve years. He was laughed at, called a madman, but faith in his destiny never wavered.

His first proposal for ships was made to Genoa out of patriotism, but that city-state, alternating between rebelling against French rule and Milanese domination, could give but little attention to the plans of a son, separated by considerable time and distance from his native land.

He then approached King John II of Portugal, who turned him down, while secretly and in breach of honorable relations, sending out men to test Columbus' theories. The Portuguese ships returned, their captains and crews terrified at the great waste of waters ahead of them, once they had left the Canaries. Columbus then saddled his faithful mule and plodded on to Spain to present his case there; many times he straddled that beast and followed the monarchs of Spain, trying to get in a word here and there between their endless ceremonies, sieges and battles against the Moors. Sometimes he must have felt that his mule understood more of what he was saying than his learned listeners.

Whether it was in Portugal, Spain, England, or France, Columbus or his brother emphasized the terrestrial gains and material riches the monarchs of those respective countries stood to gain if they would subsidize that westward voyage. Discovery of new lands is what Columbus tendered, asking only one-tenth of all profits therefrom.

He did all this with innate dignity and poise. He did not grovel, he did not whimper. This is it, he told the mighty stiff-necks of the day. I am offering you lands which will make you rich. By this time Columbus' clothes were threadbare but through no rent did anyone detect surrender or submission. By now, worry and tension had tinted the red hair of his youth into the white locks of grave concern, but that silvery crown of determination never bowed in sycophancy or servility. He knew that eventually the stiffnecks would dismount from their high horses of assumed superiority. He was certain of this, but no one else was.

It was in 1485, accompanied by his little son Diego (his wife had died) that Columbus arrived in Palos, to begin the lengthy series of negotiations that would finally bring him his vessels. He placed the boy in a Franciscan monastery, making the acquaintance of a sympathetic friar, Antonio de Marchena, who in turn introduced Columbus to the Count of Medina Celi. It was in the Alcazar in Cordoba that Columbus first had an audience with Queen Isabella, Medina Celi proving the connection at court that Columbus needed. It was in Cordoba also that Columbus met Beatriz Enriquez who became the mother, in 1488, of his second son, Ferdinand. Then began the years of alternate encouragement and frustration as Columbus sought the subsidy of the Spanish throne.

Isabella proved interested in the grand design of the Genoese mariner, and even though she was preoccupied, until 1492 as it turned out, along with her husband, Ferdinand of Aragon, with driving the last Moors out of Spain, she appointed the famous Talavera commission to evaluate the merit of the enterprise. This was to take until 1490; a subsidy from the Queen helped Columbus make ends meet during this period. Columbus was not idle while waiting for the commission's report: he tried Portugal again, but his hope of success disappeared when Bartholomew Dias returned in 1488 from the first successful rounding of the Cape of Good Hope, and the court at Lisbon undertook to reach the Indies by the longer route east around Africa. Columbus sent his brother Bartholomew to the courts of England and France with no success.

In 1490 the Talavera commission turned thumbs down: the ocean was too wide, no ship could ever return. The following year he was turned down again by another commission appointed by the sympathetic Isabella, possibly because his demands had grown too high. Then, early in 1492, the last Moorish stronghold, Granada, fell to the joint sovereigns, and Isabella now felt free to sponsor, partly from her private purse, the daring argosy. She was strongly influenced in granting her consent by Luis de Santangel, Ferdinand's receiver of ecclesiastical revenues. Columbus was already on his way to France to make a new plea there, having despaired of getting his ships from Spain, when he was overtaken by the Queen's messenger two leagues from the camp of Santa Fe, near Granada.

Finally, on April 19, 1492, the agreement between Christopher Columbus and the joint sovereigns was signed and sealed. It awarded Columbus ten per cent of the wealth which would accrue from the "lands and continents" he might discover. There was more, as their majesties declared in a document addressed directly to Columbus:

"Whereas you, Cristobal Colon, are setting forth by our command . . . to discover and acquire certain islands and mainland in the ocean sea . . . it is just and reasonable that, since you are exposing yourself to this danger in our service, you be rewarded therefore . . . it is our will and pleasure that you the said Cristobal Colon after you have discovered and acquired the said islands and mainland . . . or any of them, shall be our Admiral of the said islands and mainland which you may thus discover and acquire, and shall be empowered henceforward to call and entitle yourself Don Cristobal Colon, and his heirs and successors forever may be so entitled, and enjoy the offices of Admiral of the Ocean Sea, Viceroy and Governor of the said islands and mainland." (*Admiral of the Ocean Sea,* by Samuel Eliot Morison, Boston: Little Brown & Co., 1942, p. 105)

Columbus was provided with a letter of introduction to the Grand Khan of Cathay from the Spanish sovereigns, as well as two "to whom it may concern" type letters, on which Columbus could later add the name of any oriental potentate he happened to come across.

The town of Palos was ordered to provide Columbus with ships and men. Aided in the negotiations by Father Juan Perez, Columbus secured three vessels, as well as the invaluable assistance of the Pinzon family, leading shippers of Palos. Martin Alonso Pinzon commanded the *Pinta,* a caravel of 50 tons, 18 men. His brother Vicente Yanez Pinzon commanded the *Nina,* a 40 ton caravel, 18 men (a third brother, Francisco, was an officer aboard the *Pinta*). The flagship of the little fleet was the *Santa Maria,* a decked ship of 100 tons, 52 men, under the command of Columbus himself, and with its owner, Juan de la Cosa, aboard.

There was no crowding and jostling at the recruiting stations along the waterfront for positions on the ships riding at anchor in the little harbor of Palos, set to sail into the mists of the future. Apart from the very obvious risk in shipping on a voyage into the unknown, superstitions were rife in those days—of sea monsters, water spouts, heedless winds and dead calms. Nevertheless, it is the history of mankind that when a leader is bold enough, his daring infects the followers. Still, here and there an inducement was offered to stimulate daring. It is recorded that three youths who had been implicated in an accessory-after-the-fact murder charge were released so that they could ship with Columbus, and thereby they participated in the greatest sea adventure of all time.

At 8 a.m. on August 3, 1492, the little fleet weighed anchor and headed out to sea, the hearts of 88 men athrob, their minds awhirl with the momentousness of the enterprise which could end in fame and riches or disaster and oblivion. An evil omen struck the fleet three days out when the *Pinta* lost her rudder and had to put in at Tenerife in the Canaries for repairs. Finally on September 6th, there was the emotional farewell to the known world, and as the promontories of the islands receded into a blur and then blended into the clouds overhanging the horizon, everyone looked to the setting sun, hoping and praying that soon it might become the rising sun of salvation, of landing and then a joyous return to home and families laden with rich tidings of discovery such as had never been experienced by man before.

Columbus knew that for a few days the men would be buoyed up by the novelty of the audacious undertaking, the exhilaration of doing what no one had done before, and the prospects of good fortune awaiting them at the end of the rainbow of their expectations, but he was aware also that if landfall was delayed, fear and foreboding would pace the decks, climb the riggings, and grumbling discontent whistle through the plunging vessels. Thus, to allay apprehension and forestall panic among his men, he kept two records of the distance traveled, one, true and accurate, for his eyes alone, the other for the crew, the latter showing a lesser distance separating them from Spain.

This doctored log kept the crew satisfied for a time, but as the days lengthened into weeks the men saw themselves as corks bobbing on the surface of a darkling sea, the space between their ship and the headed-for horizon never narrowing. Nothing on the water or in the skies assured them they were not lost in an infinite sea. Their uneasiness now began to degenerate into alarm, their alarm into grumbling and grumbling into protest, with the unspoken ugly word, mutiny, beginning to circulate among them.

In spite of their Admiral's assurances they saw signs which seemed to presage disaster. The compass, their only guarantee of orientation, was acting strangely, they were passing through endless seaweed whose apparent thickness might hold them fast. On September 25 salvation seemed to have come when the cry of "Land!" went up at sunset, but in the light of dawn the hopes of the men vaporized, like the clouds whose deceptive shape had deluded the lookout. By the end of September, tensions and resentments mounted into crisis. There had been no rain, so the fresh water supply was rapidly dwindling and the food provisions would eventually give out. Ringleaders moved about furtively whispering to likely rebels that they had to save themselves, their master was insane and action had to be taken to avoid catastrophe. This could be accomplished by creeping up on the Admiral at night when he was studying the stars and throwing him overboard. They could then turn the ships around and, back in Spain, report the Admiral had slipped and fallen into the sea. They had already gone farther into the western sea than any previous sailors; their job was done.

The whisperings reached the Admiral who summoned the men to the quarterdeck in a hurry and with staccato firmness informed them that it was useless for them to think of murdering him because on their arrival in Spain no one would give credence to their story of his having fallen overboard and they would surely hang. Moreover, he again assured them, land could not be far away; once more he reminded them of the wealth awaiting them in the opulent Orient.

On October 7 came another false landfall, but the sinking of spirits that followed the dashing of this hope was modified by the passage of great flocks of birds over the ship, always flying southwest in their autumnal migration. Columbus followed the flight of the birds, certain that this would soon bring him within sight of land, but even avian clues flying overhead and vegetable clues floating on the sea failed to assuage the fears of the sailors. By October 9, according to an unconfirmed report, Columbus had to promise the two captains of the other ships, the Pinzon brothers, and Juan de la Cosa, that he would turn back if land were not sighted within three days.

By October 11 the great quantity of floating vegetation, the slight change in coloration of the water, and the pattern of the winds all confirmed Columbus in his belief that land must be imminent. So sure was he that land would be sighted that very night that he put a special watch on, and added a suit of velvet to the bonus to be awarded to whoever might shout the fateful tidings. (The overeagerness which led to the previous false landfalls had caused Columbus to cut in half this bonus if its recipient had mistakenly sighted land prior to its true discovery.) At 10 p.m. Columbus himself thought he saw a light, and twice again (a fire on shore? nobody knows).

At 2 a.m. on the morning of Friday October 12 Rodrigo de Triana, a lookout aboard the *Pinta,* sailing in the lead, became the first European known to see any part of the New World. He sang out *"Tierra!"* and the sighting was immediately confirmed by Martin Pinzon and a cannon fired as a pre-arranged signal. After 35 days on a sea never traversed by man before, this most portentous of all odysseys had reached its goal.

After the hours of nearly delirious anticipation, the light of morning permitted the three vessels to approach closely enough for them to see people gathered on the shore. The crew chanting the "Te Deum" and thanking Heaven for their safety and success, Columbus went ashore in the *Santa Maria*'s landing boat. The Pinzon brothers, in the small boats of their respective ships, the *Pinta* and the *Nina,* followed. Don Cristobal Colon, now Admiral of the Ocean Sea, Viceroy and Governor, richly attired, himself carried the royal standard.

Ashore, surrounded by the startled but silent and timid natives, Columbus and a large part of his crew first erected a crucifix, then prostrated themselves before it, thanking God and kissing the earth. Then Columbus arose and took possession of the island he had discovered in the name of Ferdinand and Isabella, naming the place San Salvador. The island, one of the Bahamas, was known as Guanahani by the Indians and was later called Watlings Island, but has since been renamed San Salvador. Those among the crew whose faith had run out so far from the end of the voyage begged the forgiveness of Columbus.

The exhilaration at the discovery Christopher Columbus had made can barely be appreciated today; nothing like it can happen in our lifetime. Even a landing of men on the moon, however scientifically significant, would fail to equal the importance of the landfall of October 12, 1492, because the existence and characteristics of the moon are already known, and it can never be more than a lonely outpost of research, never a home for man.

San Salvador was the gateway to a hemisphere; the key lay in the mind and heart of one man.

Chapter 18

MAINLAND

The astonishment of the Taino Indians at the strange garments, beards and fair complexions of their visitors was more than matched by the interest taken by the white men in the gold nose or ear pendants worn by the Indians. Sign language indicated to the white men that the gold came from a country to the south, and that is where Columbus ventured next. Two other attributes of the natives caught the attention of the Spaniards: their nakedness, and, later, their habit of inhaling the smoke of a burning weed. Only the latter attribute was suitable for export, and it was soon to become, and remain, the basis for one of the New World's principal boons to the old: tobacco.

With seven of the natives on board as interpreters, Columbus headed south. He had arrived, he thought, in the Indies; the Great Khan could not be far off, and the gold and jewels and silks and spices of the East were within his grasp. So little known was the Orient of the fifteenth century to European geographers that Columbus was to persist in this understandable error, always expecting to find his way past these islands to the mainland of Asia. Only the round-the-world expedition begun by the Portuguese Ferdinand Magellan (1480–1521) and completed in 1522, after the death of the leader in the Philippines, revealed the vast extent of the Pacific Ocean and the geographical separateness of the American lands Columbus had discovered, and by that time Columbus, too, had departed this life.

Columbus' ships sailed to Long Island, Crooked Island and others in the Bahamas and saw the coast of Cuba on October 27.

Always the source of the gold which the friendly natives wore, as ornament, proved elusive. So sure were the Spaniards that fabulous wealth was theirs for the plucking, so obliging the natives in directing the voyagers from island to island to find their gold, that impatience got the better of Martin Pinzon, and he sailed the *Pinta* far ahead of the other two vessels to reach the rainbow's end before anyone else. Columbus, with his two remaining vessels, sailed east in early December, and soon discovered the island he called Hispaniola. Today it embraces the Dominican Republic and Haiti.

Columbus also found on Hispaniola the source of the gold so abundantly worn by the Indians, and met a friend in Guacanagarí, the *cacique* or chief of the country, with whom Columbus exchanged visits of state.

On December 24, 1492, Columbus had every reason to feel a sparkle in his eye and a joyous tread in his stride. All the heartaches of his frustrations and humiliations of the past had been healed by the balm of vindication. He had triumphantly proved the correctness of all he had urged for twelve long years. He stood at the bow of his valiant *Santa Maria* catching the iridescent spray as she cleaved her way through the turquoise waters of the enchanting Caribbean. Feeling himself the personification of every detail of his grand enterprise, he supervised every movement of navigation and exploration. In the brilliant sunshine of the tropics he smiled in noting that today was Christmas Eve. At eleven that night he realized that he had not slept for 48 hours. He directed Juan de la Cosa, the officer of the watch, to take over and he retired to his cabin. We can imagine the ecstasy of this deeply religious man as he contemplated the birth of his Saviour Jesus Christ. After a felicitous prayer of thanksgiving he fell into a deep slumber, only to be awakened in an hour or two by shouts of disaster. The *Santa Maria* had run aground!

Juan de la Cosa, in defiance of every rule of maritime safety, had relinquished his responsibility as officer of the deck to the helmsman and went to sleep. The helmsman, in his turn, gave the tiller over to an inexperienced boy who allowed the vessel to run on to a coral reef which punctured the hull and the sea rushed in. The Admiral, on deck in a lightning flash, ordered La Cosa to lighten the vessel by taking the anchor and cable into the ship's boat, but La Cosa, once he had climbed down the ladder into the small boat, rowed away to the *Nina*. The seams of the *Santa Maria* opened and she was doomed.

Intense as was this calamity, Columbus did not allow it to impede the progress of his great mission. With tears in his eyes for this brave vessel of the deep which had carried him across the seas he ordered her timbers taken ashore to build a fort which he called Villa de la Navidad (Christmas Town). And here on Hispaniola, rose the first settlement of white men in the Americas. He left 38 men at the little outpost, under Diego de Harana, with articles to barter for gold and orders to treat the Indians well.

Columbus had now transferred his flag to the *Nina* and on January 4, 1493, he sailed west in the tiny ship along the north coast of the island. He finally caught up with the renegade *Pinta* and a reconciliation was effected with Martin Pinzon. On January 16 they set sail for Spain. Aboard the ship were several Indians, gold and agricultural specimens as proof of discovery.

The return voyage was probably one of the most hazardous crossings in the chronicles of the stormy Atlantic. That the tiny vessel could have survived in the towering, battering waves which all but engulfed her is one of the greatest tributes that can be paid to the seamanship of her master. When one recalls the buffetings of the 900-foot, 46,000-ton *Michelangelo* in the Atlantic tempest of April, 1966, a super liner equipped with every modern device, yet suffering a smashed and mangled superstructure with the loss of three lives, one can only wonder how the *Nina*, of 40 tons burden, with an overall length of only 65 feet and a beam of 20 feet, ever managed to stay afloat. If one wants a picture of the cauldron of shrieking winds, pitching seas and homicidal waves through which Columbus took the *Nina* he must read Columbus' journal of the voyage (New York: Clarkson N. Potter, 1960), a sample of which I give here:

> "This night the wind increased and the waves were
> terrible, one meeting another, so that they crossed and

held back the ship, which could not go forward or come out of the midst of them, and they broke over her. Seeing the danger was great, he [Columbus] began to run before the wind where it bore, as there was no other recourse . . . The sun having risen, the wind and sea were greater, the cross waves more terrible. He set only the mainsail and carried it low, in order that the ship might get out from among the waves which crossed, and threatened to sink her."

The ship was short of ballast because the stores of food and water were consumed, so he filled the casks with sea water. He agonized that the news of his great discovery might never become known in Europe.

"It seemed to him that the great desire which he had to bring this momentous news and to show that he had proved a truth-teller in what he had said and had offered to discover, inspired him with the greatest fear he would not achieve this."

He thought of his two boys in school at Cordoba, "for he would leave them orphaned of father and mother in a strange land, and that the Sovereigns would not know the services he had rendered to them on that voyage and the most favourable news which he was bearing to them, so that they might be moved to succour his sons . . . After sunset, he navigated on his course to the east. There came a squall which tore all the sails, and he saw himself in great peril; but God willed to deliver them . . . He made 60 miles before the sails were torn; afterwards they went with bare poles, owing to the great storm of wind and sea which from two sides broke over them."

With horror that his discovery would be buried at sea with him, he wrote out the story on two leaves of parchment, sealed it in a cask and tossed it into the raging seas, hoping it might reach European shores. The barrel apparently never made land, but Columbus did, finally arriving safely at Saint Mary's in the Azores.

Another storm and Columbus had to choose between trying to reach Palos or put in at a Portuguese port, running the risk of offending the Spanish sovereigns for having first landed on the soil of their hereditary rivals. Columbus determined that nothing further should jeopardize the successful completion of his mission and he dropped anchor in the Tagus, Lisbon's river. Here he confronted another embarrassment. King John, receiving Columbus, was torn between disbelief that Columbus had found a short way to the Indies, and jealousy of Spain if Columbus was telling the truth. However, once exposed to the evidence of gold and strange natives, the King concealed as best he could his chagrin in having rejected Columbus' original bid for sponsorship. He honored him with a reception and assured him a safe journey on his remaining way to Spain.

On March 15, 1493, the *Nina* arrived at Palos, its original point of departure. (Martin Pinzon arrived at a northern Spanish port at about the same time, and died a few days later.) Columbus was received as a hero, the church bells ringing out the joyous welcome. However, the great royal triumphal celebration took place at Barcelona, the seat of the court. Bringing in a procession of men laden with the strange flora and fauna he had collected, the all-important gold, and his retinue of Indians, Columbus kneeled before his sovereigns Ferdinand and Isabella, who asked him to rise and commanded him to be seated in their presence. He then told them his exciting story and revealed his proofs of land in the west.

The title of Don was now officially conferred on Columbus, the promised privileges confirmed, and the right granted him to add the coats of arms of the kingdoms of Castile and Leon to that of his family, with emblems signifying his discoveries.

If Bjarni and Leif ever got to America, they got here by accidents, by winds which they fought, by currents which prevailed against their wishes. And if they got here, they cannot have understood what they saw. Bjarni never came back; Leif never returned. Their stay on this continent, if it occurred at all, was that of a whale dashed ashore in a storm and at the first lull in the tempest takes to the sea again, stunned by his momentary and forced terrestrial immobility and hoping never to be caught in such a violent elemental turmoil again.

Columbus not only returned, he retraced his oceanic steps on three more momentous voyages, each successive voyage adding new lands to man's conquest over the unknown. With Columbus' discoveries, the Western Hemisphere exploded into a seething arena of colonization. Europe itself erupted with exploratory projects.

Columbus' second voyage was the largest in size of his four. He led a fleet of 17 vessels, including the *Nina,* carrying 1200 persons. The expedition had the joint purpose of colonizing the new lands and converting the natives to Christianity, a small delegation of priests accompanying the colonists.

On November 3, 1493, the fleet sighted the island of Dominica. In the succeeding weeks new names were added to the map of the world almost as fast, figuratively, as the ink could flow to write them. Columbus cruised and explored the Lesser Antilles—Guadeloupe, Montserrat, Antigua, St. Kitts and Nevis, among other islands—and also brought Jamaica, the Virgin Islands and Puerto Rico into the history of the civilized world. A great misfortune awaited him when he returned to Hispaniola, the first of a number that would blight what should have been his years of triumph. His fort of Navidad had been wiped out by the Indians, with no survivors. A new colony, Isabela, was promptly begun on the same island, and before his return, in 1494, Columbus left his brother Bartholomew in charge.

On May 30, 1498, Columbus sailed on his third voyage with two fleets comprising six vessels. This time he headed further south for the mainland of Asia. What he did find, after a first landfall at Trinidad, was nothing less than South America. On August 5, 1498, he discovered the mainland of the American continent, landing on the coast of Venezuela.

For several days he coasted the seaboard, and when he noted the vast volumes of water pouring from the Orinoco into the sea, he realized the truly continental character of this present discovery, but he thought it was adjacent to Asia. After some further exploring he set sail for Hispaniola, anticipating with pleasure the progress he expected to find in the colony. He was to be sorely disappointed. Cliques and bitter rivalries among the Spaniards had degenerated into open rebellion against Columbus' brother Bartholomew.

Back in Spain, Columbus' enemies had prevailed on King Ferdinand, who had never cherished, as did the Queen, a warm feeling for Columbus, to appoint a governor with full sovereign powers over Hispaniola. This governor turned out to be the ruthless Francisco de Bobadilla who, upon arrival in the Spanish colony, accused Columbus and his two brothers, Diego and Bartholomew, with misgovernment, placed them all in chains and ordered them back to Spain for trial.

On the return voyage, the captain of the vessel offered to remove Columbus' chains, but he refused, stating he would wear them in the presence of the King to remind him, as he had said in a letter to a lady at court:

> ". . . by the divine will I have placed under the sovereignty of the King and Queen an Other World, whereby Spain, which was reckoned poor, is become the richest of countries." (*Christopher Columbus, Mariner,* by Samuel Eliot Morison, Boston: Little, Brown & Co., 1955)

The poignant appearance of the Great Discoverer in chains brought cries of anguish from the Spanish populace and the King ordered the fetters struck. He also restored to Columbus his titles, repudiated Bobadilla's proceedings, and authorized a Fourth Voyage, to start in 1502.

The King's intimates managed, however, to assign to Columbus in this fourth voyage four antiquated, badly constructed, leaky ships. With them he explored the Atlantic coast of Central America, looking in vain for the passage that would bring him directly to the Asiatic continent. Two of the ships he had to abandon on the way, and then, in the last extremity of peril, while nearing the coast of Jamaica, with his decks awash, he sailed full tilt toward shore, running his now useless vessels on to the beach. They were to become his home and prison for a year.

Here, in addition to the fear that he had been forgotten, deserted and never to be rescued, other calamities assailed Columbus: mutiny, food shortage, and menacing Indians.

These last two problems were dealt with by a famous stratagem. Knowing that a total eclipse of the moon was due a certain evening, Columbus summoned the Indian leaders and told them that the God of the white men would darken the moon that night. The moon actually was eclipsed, the natives frightened out of their wits by the heavenly omen until Columbus promised to restore the light by interceding with his God on behalf of the Indians, contingent, of course, upon their promising to feed the white men. The stratagem worked: the white men got their meals; the Indians got back their moon.

The career of Columbus was now itself in eclipse. The glory of his first triumphant return was long past; Isabella, without whose good will none of his voyages would have come to pass, died shortly after Columbus' return in 1504; and Ferdinand was indifferent to his welfare.

At this time of his life, when he should have been living in comfort, affluence and even luxury, Columbus occupied a modest house in Valladolid, ill, half-forgotten and neglected by those to whom he had brought renown, riches and glory beyond the dreams of avarice. His attempt to settle his claims upon the throne met with failure, possibly because of his just refusal to renounce the titles he had been granted.

Throughout the entire tenancy of man's estate, Columbus had never known ease or diversion. His entire life was dedicated to God's work and duty. For twelve years or more, in the freshness of manhood, when his surpassing abilities could have gained him personal riches, he tramped the highways knocking at inhospitable doors like a mendicant, seeking the means and the ships with which to discover a world. Then, over a span of thirteen years, he plowed heavy and angry waters in infirm vessels, subsisting mostly on salt pork, hardtack and dried peas. In all his journeyings he lacked proper food, medicines, doctors, adequate sleeping facilities and shelter. The many hundreds of days and nights of exposure to nature's rebukes in storm at sea, in jungle, on uncharted beach, and perhaps the nearly unceasing exposure to man's rebukes—recalcitrant monarchs, mutinous crews, threatening Indians, gold-greedy malcontents—all conspired to sap the vitality from his tall and well-formed body. He died May 20, 1506.

Chapter 19

COLUMBIANA

The greatness of Columbus, so obvious from the vantage point of later generations, could commend itself to few others while he lived. The extent of the world that lay behind the curtain he had raised, and the extent of the riches and empire they would give to Spain, were both revealed only in the generation after his death. Columbus was well aware that he had reached, on his third voyage, a land of continental proportions, mistaken though he necessarily was about its proximity to Asia; and he was well aware of the potentialities for wealth and glory that lay in this land for the crown of Spain. But the small minds that measured a continent by the number of gold mines that accommodating natives could point to, cheated Columbus of the full glory of his discovery in his lifetime. And an ironic twist of fate saw the new continent named after the wrong man, one Amerigo Vespucci, in the year following Columbus' death.

Truth cannot be contained forever, it must break out of confinement and light the world. So was it with the truth of the achievement of Columbus. But there is a type of mind that always prefers the esoteric theory that destroys a popular image and gives its proponent a comforting smugness and feeling of pseudo-sophistication, while eschewing the obvious truth believed by the multitudes. Thus, in modern times, we have seen studious efforts to "prove" that the plays of Shakespeare were actually written by someone else, with ciphers and misinterpretation exhibited in pitiful defiance of the overwhelming documentary evidence that the man from Stratford was the

author of the works that bore his name. And more and more
voices have sought, in recent years, to call attention to themselves by shrieking belittlement of the man from Genoa.

It began, quietly enough, in 1837 when Carl Christian
Rafn, a Danish scholar, published a book on the Icelandic sagas
which burdened these medieval admixtures of fact and fancy
with the weight of literal interpretation. The intriguing suggestiveness, the coy allusiveness of the sagas, as more writers turned
their attention to them, jelled into proof positive that Leif Ericson had discovered America before Columbus. Following Rafn,
hints became history, and the single paragraph about a sailor
named Leif Ericson being blown off course became the holy
writ of a new faith (the low regard that even most of the Vinland proponents have for the *Greenlanders' Saga* had ousted
Bjarni Herjolfsson from estimation as a discoverer of America).
As for Rafn's book itself, Arthur Middleton Reeves, in *The
Finding of Wineland the Good,* found fault with "the heedless
confusing of all of the material bearing directly or indirectly
upon his theme, the failure to winnow the sound historical
material from that which is unsubstantiated . . . many dubious
theories and hazard conjectures."

As long as the truth and the landfalls that lay behind the
Norse sagas are anybody's guess, no one need be faulted for
making an educated guess as to whether or not the Vinland tales
reflect a real chancing upon our shores. I object only when conjecture is waved in the public's eye and splashed on the pages of
school texts with the panoply of proven fact. When one forgets
the qualifying phrases that must clothe fanciful speculation if it
is not to appear indecent in public, the result can be as eccentric as a recent book that strains to become the bible of the
"Who was Columbus anyhow?" cult: *They All Discovered
America,* by Charles Michael Boland (Garden City: Doubleday,
1961). The book promises, and delivers, no less than nineteen
groups of pre-Columbian discoverers of America, including
Phoenicians, Etruscans, Chinese, Welsh, Portuguese, and, of
course, Norse. As for Columbus, he is airily dismissed by the author's assurance to the reader that he was simply following

where he knew others had gone, betting on a sure thing as it were (it is too bad Columbus didn't have a copy of Boland's book aboard to quell the mutiny). Praise for Columbus' courage, says this book, is "so much balderdash." As for the author's "proofs," they are just as convincing as you would expect in a book offering nineteen discoverers of America. One feels that if some bones were offered to the author as the skeleton of a uniped, they would be solemnly exhibited in the next edition.

But while we can find some amusement in such phantasizing, the presentation to the world of the Vinland Map is another matter, and quite a serious one. Whatever conclusions the staff of the Yale Library may have come to regarding the map's genuineness and significance, there can be no doubt but that the melodramatic bravura attending its announcement constituted a breach of the trust between the American public and Yale. In a publicity campaign seemingly quarterbacked by a team consisting of P. T. Barnum and Machiavelli, Columbus Day itself was exploited to ram down the public's throat the "news" that Leif Ericson (with Bjarni now elevated to equal billing) discovered America and that the final verification was the cartographic grotesquerie concurrently published by the Yale University Press.

I thought an opposing voice should be heard, and so I wrote this book to remind as many readers as I could find that the case for Viking landfalls in North America is not proven and that, whatever solution to the mystery of the sagas one prefers, the true meaning of the word "discovery" excludes anyone before Columbus from usurping the title of the great Genoese mariner: Discoverer of America.

Webster's International Dictionary, illustrating the meaning of the verb "discover," says: "One discovers what existed before, but had remained unknown," and adds "as Columbus discovered America." Leif's Vinland may have existed before, but it is still unknown. Where was it? Who got there first? Who came afterward and why didn't they stay? Columbus added to the world's knowledge; the ancient Norsemen, or rather their present-day champions, add to the world's riddles. The splendid achievements of the Scandinavians, ancient and modern, do not need the gratuitous addition of an unearned discovery to excite our profound admiration.

The *Encyclopaedia Britannica*, 1965 edition, begins its article on Christopher Columbus with these words: "COLUMBUS, CHRISTOPHER (Sp. Cristóbal Colón) (1451–1506), discoverer of the new world."

The *Encyclopedia Americana* starts its counterpart article: "COLUMBUS, CHRISTOPHER, Discoverer of America."

The *Encyclopedia International,* another great reference work, uses the identical words, and so does the *World Book Encyclopedia* say "Columbus, Christopher, The Discoverer of America."

In his Pulitzer Prize-winning two-volume *Columbus, Admiral of the Ocean Sea,* Samuel Eliot Morison, one of the greatest living authorities on Columbus, extols the Genoese as a discoverer, not as one who followed, not as one who copies, not as one brave only after the first dangers had been faced, but as the first man to conquer the tempest, to pave the highway to the setting sun for others to follow along it. There was nothing fortuitous about Columbus' enterprise: for years he had sought the ships to put his plans of discovery into effect.

These words conclude Admiral Morison's classic tribute:

> "One only wishes that the Admiral might have been afforded the sense of fulfillment that would have come from foreseeing all that flowed from his discoveries; that would have turned all the sorrows of his last years to joy. The whole history of the Americas stems from the four voyages of Columbus; and as the Greek city-states looked back to the death-less gods as their founders, so today a score of independent nations and dominions unite in homage to Christopher the stout-hearted son of Genoa, who carried Christian civilization across the Ocean Sea."

Many of those who assert a pre-Columbian discovery of America add, in a patronizing manner, that they are quite will-

ing to concede to Columbus credit for his role in the development of the Americas. This is like sparing a little credit for
Thomas Edison for his "role" in the development of the electric
light. If Columbus hadn't revealed America to Europe, someone else would have, sooner or later, they say (and someone else
would have invented the electric light if Edison hadn't . . . we
hope). But it was Columbus who did, Columbus who alone laid
the foundation on which the entire structure of modern America rests.

Perhaps the happiest summation of the argument for rec-
ognizing only Columbus as the discoverer of America was given
by Jimmy Durante, as quoted in Samuel Eliot Morison's review
of the Vinland-Tartar book in the New York *Times:*

> "Although not 'poisonally' acquainted with Co-
> lumbus, said the 'Schnozzle,' he did know that Colum-
> bus on arrival 'played only to Indians—there were no
> Norwegians in the audience!' "

The Philadelphia *Inquirer* said something very similar in
an editorial: "If the efforts to downgrade Columbus' discovery
of America keep up you will have to wonder how the great
navigator ever got through the crowds waiting for him on the
docks."

But the voices of deprecation and patronization are a thin
and piping counterpoint to the daily repetition of the countless
names that are the most eloquent tribute to the place Columbus
holds in the hearts of our people: the District of Columbia, cap-
ital of our nation; Columbia University; the Republic of Co-
lombia; Colon in Panama; the cities and towns named Columbus, in Arkansas, Georgia, Indiana, Kansas, Kentucky, Mississippi, Montana, Nebraska, New Jersey, New Mexico, North
Carolina, North Dakota, Ohio, Pennsylvania, Texas, and Wis-
consin. And the cities and towns named Columbia, in Alabama,
Connecticut, Florida, Illinois, Kentucky, Louisiana, Mississippi,
Missouri, New Jersey, North Carolina, Pennsylvania, South
Carolina, South Dakota, Tennessee, Utah, and Virginia . . .

and the Columbia River. Over thirty other towns or other geographical entities such as mountains, lakes, rivers, etc., bear the
name of Columbus or a derivative therefrom. The strains of
Hail, Columbia and *Columbia, the Gem of the Ocean* add
music to the sound of tribute.

It is significant that the leading Roman Catholic laymen's
organization in the United States (over a million members),
dedicated to religious ideals and civic usefulness, has shown its
appreciation of and gratitude to the discoverer by adopting the
name The Knights of Columbus.

The 400th anniversary of Columbus' discovery was celebrated by the magnificent World's Columbian Exposition in
Chicago, and by the issuance by the United States of a superb
series of commemorative postage stamps, the first our country
produced, each bearing a scene from the discoverer's life. The
United States also minted a Columbian half dollar, one of
which I proudly carry in my pocket. Columbus Day is celebrated by designation in the various states, rather than as a national holiday. Many of us are pledged to persuade the Congress
to make October 12 a legal holiday throughout the country, and
the insult of October 12 of 1965 only renews our determination.
Many cities and towns in Italy, Spain, Canada and Latin America join in the celebration with church services and festivities, to
honor the man who made what Samuel Eliot Morison has called
(in *Christopher Columbus, Mariner*) "the most spectacular
and far-reaching geographical discovery in recorded human history."

His remains are now sepulchered in the cathedral at Santo
Domingo, in the Dominican Republic. There I was privileged
to visit him one day. I knelt at his tomb in the Cathedral of
Santo Domingo and paid my own silent tribute to this unparal-
leled figure who gave mankind a world named for another,
riches beyond measure in return for chains and scorn, and,
above all, hope, opportunity, and inspiration without limit.

INDEX

ABOUT THE AUTHOR

Justice Michael A. Musmanno of the Pennsylvania Supreme Court was born of Italian immigrant parents in Stowe
Township, near Pittsburgh, where he still makes his home.
He is a graduate of five universities, holding seven earned
degrees. One of these he won at the University of Rome,
where he pursued studies for his doctorate in jurisprudence
while intensively researching the life of Christopher Columbus, his inspirational hero from childhood days.

His intimate knowledge of the events in the epochal
career of the Genoese navigator, combined with a zestful and
unquenchable enthusiasm on the subject, has led to his being
chosen on numerous occasions to debate—on radio, television,
public platform and in print—against the theorists who claim
pre-Columbian discoveries of America. The Pittsburgh *Post-
Gazette* recently called Justice Musmanno Columbus' "most
vehement and voluble champion."

The author saw service in World War I in the United
States Army, and, during World War II, served as naval aide,
with the rank of Lieutenant Commander, to General Mark
W. Clark, commanding the Allied Armies in Italy. Twice
wounded in action, he was decorated many times and presently holds the rank of Rear Admiral (Ret. U.S.N.R.).

President Harry S. Truman appointed him to the International Military Tribunal for the War Crimes Trials in
Nuremberg, where he presided over the Einsatzgruppen trial,
called "the biggest murder trial in history." The decisions he

wrote, bringing the Law of Humanity into the international code of jurisprudence, prompted Gideon Hausner, former Attorney General of Israel, and prosecutor of Adolf Eichmann, to declare in his recent book *Justice in Jerusalem,* "Michael Angelo Musmanno, whose Italian origin is clearly carved on his distinguished Roman face, rendered world-famous decisions, combining highest judicial standards with deep moral convictions, couched in language of a beauty rarely equaled in legal records."

Although the author of more than a dozen books, Justice Musmanno took special delight in writing *Columbus WAS First,* since it called into play such a large number of his enthusiasms and talents: his devotion to Columbus, love of the sea and its epic adventures, extraordinary ability in analyzing documentary evidence, and, especially satisfying to one who spent so many years as a battling attorney, the opportunity to punch great gaping holes in the supposedly "perfect" case of a confident opposition.